MARKETPLACE MISSIONARIES

WHERE WILL YOUR COWORKERS SPEND ETERNITY?

TOM DARBY

publication. Further, the publisher does not have any control over and does not assume any responsibility for author or third-party websites or their content.

19 20 21 22 23 — 9 8 7 6 5 4 3 2 1

Printed in the United States of America

❋ Created with Vellum

CONTENTS

[1]
WHERE WILL THEY SPEND ETERNITY?

THE PHONE RANG and startled me out of my sleep. "Hello," I managed to say, though groggy. Trying to get my bearings, I looked at my alarm clock and noticed it was about one in the morning.

"Tom, I'm sorry to bother you," the voice said in my ear. "I got your name and number from the guard shack at work. I'm calling to let you know that my brother, Dave, died of a heart attack tonight."

I can't say that I instantly knew who I was speaking to, but from what the voice said, I started to put together that it was the brother of one of the employees I had spoken to at lunch the previous day. I could hear the pain and disbelief in the brother's voice as he shared this news with me.

"I'm sorry for your loss. If there's anything I can do, just let me know." I offered the brother the usual hollow words of comfort.

He thanked me, and then we both hung up.

My body was numb with shock. Devastated, I lay there in the dark. When I had spoken to Dave the day before, he had asked me how to accept Jesus into his heart, but I had put off answering him.

Oh, God, what did I do? Why did I rush out to that other meeting? Why didn't I stop to answer him? The thoughts and questions were screaming in my head. Going back to sleep was anything but possible.

REMEMBERING

When I had started my position as a manufacturing management trainee, my first assignment was to supervise an area on our shop floor. My time in this position helped clarify any wonderings I may have had about why this position offered so much more pay than the other positions I had been offered.

On my first day, I was taken down to the area in the shop where I would be working and was handed off to the manager of that area. As I approached his office, he waved me in. I stepped in and closed the door. The smile left his face immediately, and he then let me know I was expected to be at work prior to six each morning and he was the only person in the department who would be wearing a tie, so I should remove mine and leave it in his office.

The language he used while telling me all of this was quite salty, and his tone was quite loud. I am sure my eyes were as big as saucers. I can remember thinking, *Oh, no. What have I gotten myself into?*

Though I could have guessed it, I later discovered that this manager was a former military man, bull-of-the-woods type of guy.

Next, I was introduced to three other supervisors who worked in the area with me. We all reported to the same bull-of-the-woods manager. They quickly tried to help me get up to speed as they knew it would be the only way I would survive in this position.

Every day, I would prepare to be grilled by my manager about my employees' performance and different issues that were going on in my area. He seemed to be less than enthused that an engineering graduate was being put in his area as part of a new manufacturing management training program, but he was a guinea pig no differently than I was as this was the first time the company had done something like this.

At twenty-two years old, I was the youngest person in a department of seventy people. In addition to dealing with the drill-sergeant boss, I was also having to supervise and lead men and women who were as old as my grandparents. It took a lot of hard work and the application of some interpersonal skills I had learned from my parents. Eventually, I earned the respect of the people who reported to me as well as the man to whom I was reporting.

One of the supervisors I worked with in those beginning years was Dave, a former Detroit police officer. He was a kind man who took a liking to me and tried to help me navigate my relationship with our boss. After about three months, I was finally getting my feet on the ground and had gotten a pretty good grasp for my area of responsibility. Still, nearly every day, my manager would come storming through the department, loudly peppering me with questions.

One day, Dave sat me down and said, "You know, he will not stop doing this to you until you get back in his face the same way he is getting in yours. He is testing you."

A few days later, the manager started in on me about something I knew far more about than he did, and his facts were not correct. I took a deep breath as it was not in my nature to be loud or overly aggressive with people. I preferred to talk calmly and in private, but that day, I had had enough!

When he finished with his aggressive questioning, I got right up in his face and without yelling but in an heightened tone told him exactly where he was wrong and what the facts were. Much to my surprise, that bull-of-the-woods manager smiled, turned, and walked away. From that point on, our relationship changed. His demeanor and tone changed with how he approached me each day.

After a while, Dave noticed I would sometimes not eat lunch with everyone in the cafeteria. In fact, I would leave during our lunchtime. One day, Dave asked me where I was going. I told him I was going to a Bible study and asked him if he wanted to come. He smiled and politely declined, but I could feel him watching me as I left. I thought that he must have begun to notice the changes that had been happening in me.

My relationship with my manager had gotten better but was still difficult to navigate, so I mentioned something to the man who was discipling me in Christ at the time. He was also the leader of the lunchtime Bible studies. He asked me if I had prayed for my manager.

Pray for him? I thought. *You have to be kidding me! I want to punch him in the nose most of the time.*

As my spiritual mentor, he pointed me to Matthew 5:43–48:

> "You have heard that it was said, 'Love your neighbor and hate your enemy.' But I tell you, love your enemies and pray for those who persecute you, that you may be children of your Father in heaven. He causes his sun to rise on the evil and the good, and sends rain on the righteous and the unrighteous. If you love those who love you, what reward will you get? Are not even the tax collectors doing that? And if you greet only your own people, what are you doing more than others? Do not even the pagans do that? Be perfect, therefore, as your heavenly Father is perfect."

Then, he pointed me to 1 Timothy 2:1–4 about praying for my leaders:

> I urge, then, first of all, that petitions, prayers, intercession and thanksgiving be made for all people—for kings and all those in authority, that we may live peaceful and quiet lives in all godliness and holiness. This is good,

and pleases God our Savior, who wants all people to be saved and to come to a knowledge of the truth.

I was convicted by the Holy Spirit after reading these passages and thinking about how I was approaching my relationship with my manager. After I had stood up to him, the way he communicated with me was better, but our relationship was far from being peaceful, good, and healthy. I decided to take God at His Word and began to pray for my manager and our relationship. What I found was, at first, it did more to change me than it did him. My heart softened for him. I began to wonder what type of upbringing he may have had and what things he had dealt with in his life. I started trying to honor him and his position.

By the time my one year was up in his department and I had to move to my next assignment, he called me into his office and with tears in his eyes asked if I would stay. He felt he had more he could teach me. He wanted to continue working with me. I knew I needed to move on and knew God had more for me to learn and more relationships to build in other areas of the company, so I respectfully declined his offer for me to stay. I will always be thankful for that relationship and how God used that old grizzly marine to teach me how to pray for those for whom I may not normally be inclined to pray.

"WHY DON'T YOU KNOW?"

Over the next few years, I would be given the opportunity to work in different positions inside the company, continuing my training. God's favor went before me as I was given the opportunity to learn a wide range of disciplines in a very short time and build many relationships throughout the organization. I did my best to let God's light shine through how I went about my job and interacted with others. I tried to be patient and wait for the Holy Spirit to present opportunities to share my faith.

After working in four different positions in four years, I was put in a manufacturing manager's position. I was actually tasked with filling the shoes of my first boss. The bull-of-the-woods military man had recently retired. I was back where I had started, but this time around, the supervisors with whom I had been working would now work for me. My being promoted over them created issues for some of them where they felt I had not paid my dues and was too young to hold a manager's position. Many of them felt they should have received the promotion and not me.

There was one supervisor who did not feel this way. It was Dave, the former Detroit police officer who had befriended me when we worked together in this department previously. He was one of the first to congratulate me and assured me that I had his support in whatever manner I needed it. Our relationship continued to grow, and he occasionally asked me questions about God, the Bible, and church.

One day, Dave stopped by my office at lunchtime and mentioned that he had noticed I didn't swear and yell during our weekly meetings. The language on the manufacturing shop floor smacked of the former manager's language. When I spoke, I chose to do my best at leading by example with the tone and language I used. I have always believed that I do not need to yell, scream, and swear to get my point across. I can be just as or more effective using a direct, honest, and calm approach while interacting with those with whom I work.

A couple weeks later after Dave had talked to me about my not swearing or yelling, I arrived at my office to find a framed notice hanging on the wall. My former police officer supervisor had made a sign proclaiming, "This Is A No-Swear Zone. Violators Will Be Fined."

Dave was a man of his word, and he was well-suited to mete out the fines and collect them. When he had collected enough in fines, he would spend the money on doughnuts and bring them to our meetings. At first, we ate a lot of doughnuts, but over time the mood and language in the meetings changed. I didn't have to complain or say a word, thanks to Dave.

God continued to provide me with opportunities to share and pray with others at my workplace. The conversations were not forced. I let the Holy Spirit open the doors and get the conversations going, and then I did my best to share what I felt God was leading me to share.

One day in 1992, Dave came into my office at lunchtime to talk to me. He would come in and sit down and talk to me every couple of weeks about a wide variety of things. This day his demeanor seemed a little different. He sat there with a piece of pecan pie he had purchased from the cafeteria. It sat on a Styrofoam plate, which he balanced on his lap. He used a plastic spork to scoop up his bites as he talked to me. I sat listening as I prepared for a weekly production meeting scheduled for that afternoon with the upper management of our company.

He asked me, "What does it take for me to become a Christian? Do I just pray some prayer or what?"

I had ten minutes before my production meeting would begin, so I asked him if we could have this conversation after I got back from my meeting. He smiled and said we could.

After the meeting, we both had gotten busy and never reconnected that afternoon.

It was later that very night at home when I received the phone call from Dave's brother. I remember I told my wife, Karen, that the call was someone informing me that a coworker had passed away earlier in the evening. I could not bring myself to even talk about what had transpired earlier that day. I lay there awake for the rest of the night just praying to God for a sign.

"Did Dave make a decision for Christ?" I asked Him. "Is he in heaven?"

I continued to pray and received no confirmation on whether or not the former police officer who had worked for and befriended me had made a decision to accept Christ.

A few days went by, and as the time for the funeral approached, I started to think and hope maybe someone at the funeral would mention something about a decision Dave had made. There was nothing. No one mentioned anything that helped me to know where Dave was spending eternity. This put me into a complete spiritual funk. I felt like a failure. I cried out to God, and finally I felt Him ask me, "Why don't you know?"

Those were four simple words I will never forget.

"Why don't you know?"—these words were not condemning. They were gentle words from a Father answering a child's question with a question.

On many occasions in answer to my kids or to people who work for me, I will ask them a question. Answering in this way sometimes causes them to think about something and dig deeper. This method is called the Socratic approach, asking and answering questions to stimulate critical thinking. That four-word question was my answer from God, though it was not the one I was hoping for.

THE MOST IMPORTANT THINGS IN LIFE

I know the truth: We are incapable of saving anyone, including ourselves, from eternal separation from God, which, as sinners, is what we deserve. I know that Jesus did that work on the cross some two thousand years ago. I know that He redeemed us and that salvation is a gift we only need to choose to accept and make Him Lord of our lives. Still, I wrestled with God's question and fought feelings of failure when I thought about my coworker and our interaction on the day he died. But, soon, the reality of it all became clear.

What God helped me to realize was I was not always making my relationship with Him and serving Him the most important things in my life. The words Jesus used to answer the Sadducees and Pharisees in Matthew 22 when they were testing Him lifted off the page one day as I read them:

> Love the Lord your God with all your heart and with all your soul and with all your mind. This is the first and greatest commandment. And the second is like it. Love your neighbor as yourself. All the Law and the Prophets hang on these two commandments.

> - VV. 37-40

After reading these verses, I deposited these precious words in my heart. I reconsidered the last day I spent with Dave, our conversation in my office, his desire to know how to become a Christian, and my feelings of responsibility to attend the meeting. I came to this conclusion: If I had spent fifteen minutes with him and showed up for the meeting fifteen minutes late, nobody would have thought anything of it. The meeting lasted a couple of hours, and I typically presented near the end of each meeting. Everyone would have assumed that I had been detained because I was taking care of something work related. As long as I would have arrived in time to present, there would have been no issue. The problem was I liked going to that meeting and rubbing shoulders with the leaders of the company. In the situation, I made that a priority over loving my neighbor.

I am now 100 percent sure that, if I had known the importance of the lunch talk with my coworker, I would have made it a priority to share with him exactly what the Bible says about Jesus and the finished work of the cross. What became real to me on that day in 1992 was this: We don't know what each day holds for ourselves or those with whom we come into contact. Life is fleeting.

Now listen, you who say, "Today or tomorrow we will go to this or that city, spend a year there, carry on business and make money." Why, you do not even know what will happen tomorrow. What is your life? You are a mist that appears for a little while and then vanishes.

- JAMES 4:13-14

As I had lain awake in the wee hours of the morning after the phone call from Dave's brother, I had struggled with not knowing where Dave would spend eternity. Nothing else seemed to matter in those dark remaining hours before sunrise. Everything else faded away into the recesses of my mind but Dave and where he was. I was left with the reality that so many people I was working with every day needed God's grace and mercy, that they too needed to repent and accept the eternal salvation that Jesus alone provides.

This fire and compassion I had for them was fresh on my heart. After all, I too had only four years prior to Dave's death received Christ myself. I could hardly contain the night-and-day difference Jesus had made in my life and the desire to have more of Him every day. So, I had joined the prayer groups and Bible studies in the workplace. But something changed for me there in the darkness of my room that early morning. In that moment, my view of the people around me changed. Yes, I had a new life filled with the hope of everlasting life, but what about them? Where would they spend eternity?

WHAT ABOUT YOU?

Where has God placed you? Where is your workplace, your mission field of service? Whom has He placed in that workplace with you, and do you know where they will spend eternity?

My purpose in writing this book, in sharing the story of Dave and me, is to let you know God wants you to be a missionary in your workplace. He wants to use you to reach the lost in the place you spend a third or more of almost every day of your life.

In the pages that follow, I want to share my story, how someone in my workplace influenced me toward Christ, and the ways I have seen God move in people's lives in the workplace for the past thirty-plus years.

I pray that the Holy Spirit reveals to you strategies that help you impact those you work with for Christ.

If you have already embarked on a journey as a marketplace missionary, I pray that you will find this book encouraging and helpful in making you more effective in your marketplace journey.

If you have not yet felt God's call on you to share your faith in the marketplace, I pray that the Lord of the harvest would make known to you the plans and purposes He has prepared for you and those around you.

Being prepared and willing are vital to introducing those God has placed into our sphere of influence to Jesus and an eternity spent in His presence. If we do not make a decision that we are going to share Jesus with others prior to getting these opportunities, we are far less likely to do so. The good news is this is not a journey we travel alone. Jesus assures us at the end of the Great Commission in Matthew 28:20 that He is always with us:

And surely I am with you always, to the very end of the age.

[2]
LIVING FOR MYSELF

I WAS BORN and raised in Kalamazoo, Michigan, and am the oldest of four children. I grew up with good, godly parents.

My father was raised Catholic, so in my youth, we attended the local Catholic church. Because of his upbringing, my dad's faith was more religious than relationship based.

My mom, on the other hand, was a Spirit-filled woman of God who was on fire for Jesus!

Over the years, I have watched my dad's faith transform from being religious to becoming one that is centered on a vibrant relationship with the living God. Who I am today is due, in large part, to how my parents raised me and the consistent prayers they have covered me with for decades. I thank God frequently for my parents and the impact they have had on my life.

MY MOTHER'S SHINING EXAMPLE

There are a few foundational things I have built upon when it comes to having an impact for Jesus in the marketplace. One of those foundational underpinnings was watching my mother's marketplace ministry while I grew up. She was a stay-at-home mother, and her marketplace was our neighborhood and community.

In the summers when school was out, I can remember coming downstairs every morning and seeing my mom reading her Bible and praying. She was never pushy but always willing to offer prayer for people or share about Jesus when the opportunity presented itself. People did not have to wonder where she stood when it came to having a relationship with Jesus. They knew. Helping to meet people's current needs, loving on them, and caring for them was just who she was and is.

There were times when we were at community gatherings that I remember hearing people make fun of her. They would call her a Jesus freak or overly religious. When I heard these comments, I felt all kinds of emotion: confusion, anger, embarrassment, and shame. But, as the years went by, I noticed that some of these same people who said those remarks ended up sitting at our kitchen table, asking for prayer for something that had gone terribly wrong in their lives.

My mother was a shining example of what it meant to be more concerned about where someone would spend eternity than all the other noise and gossip that floated around her at times.

CHOOSING TO LIVE FOR MYSELF

Despite witnessing all of this and knowing without any doubt who Jesus is and what He did for me, by the time I was in high school, I still chose to live for myself.

When I was preparing for my freshman year, my mom received a word from God for me. He told her that I would have great success in basketball during my senior year.

Now, you have to understand that, at this point in my life, I loved playing basketball but had not had much success. In seventh grade, I did not make the A team, which was made up of the best twenty-five players in my grade. In eighth grade, I was the last one chosen out of twenty kids for the A team.

My dad, on the other hand, was a Division 1 college football player who in high school won all-conference honors in football, basketball, and baseball. He was also named a first team all-state halfback for football. He never pushed me in sports and was not one of those overbearing parents who applied pressure to their kids to perform better. Still, I was very disappointed and felt like a failure as I couldn't help but compare myself to all of his amazing athletic accomplishments.

So, with all this, it's no wonder that, when my mom told me what God had told her, I was surprised. I wasn't even sure I was going to make the freshman team let alone have a great senior season. All I could think was, *That'll be a miracle.*

You've probably already guessed. Mom was right. I made the freshman team and went on to have a great senior season on the basketball team, where we only lost a few games. As we came into the final game of the season, we had an opportunity to win our conference championship. If we were to win this last game, and the rival team we were battling with atop the conference all year lost their game that same night, then the conference championship would by ours.

In the end, it came down to a last-second shot, which I was fortunate enough to make. The conference championship we had worked for as a team, though, eluded us as our rivals also won their game that evening. After this game, it was on to the state tournament where I made the winning basket in the first two games of that tournament. I came home to a newspaper sitting on the table with the front-page saying, "Darby Hero Again," as well as a large write-up in the sports section. This was back in the day when the newspaper was community driven and a big deal. I remember standing there thinking, *Wow! Mom really did hear from God.*

Even though, while standing there in the dining room of our home, I felt that strong tug on my heart that I know today was the Holy Spirit, I chose not to yield to it or Him. My mom had heard God regarding me and this season in my life, and God had worked what was to me a personal miracle. But I chose there and then to continue living for myself and not for Him.

I knew He died for my sins and loved me, but I was not ready to surrender my life to Him. I chose to believe the lie from the enemy that I was young and should live my life for myself because there would be plenty of time for God when I got old. I chose to believe the lie that, as long as I felt I was not hurting others, I could do what I wanted to. All that choosing to distance myself from God did was cause more anxiety in my life and less peace.

Mankind has been dealing with these lies from the enemy since Adam and Eve took a bite of that consternating fruit in the garden of Eden. God has made it clear in His Word that we have a choice to make. We can choose to accept His gift of salvation and a right relationship with Him or believe the lies of the enemy and the bondages, death, and destruction that they bring. Up until my early twenties, I had made the decision to reject God and what He had to offer me, accepting instead the lies from the enemy. Yet my mother's example had impacted me more than I even knew at the time.

[3]
LIVING FOR GOD

AFTER HIGH SCHOOL, it was off to college to study mechanical engineering. And that equated to four more years of living life for myself despite knowing Jesus had died for me. I continued to believe the lie that I would be happier doing life my way and waiting until sometime in the future when I was old, you know like thirty, to surrender my life to God.

My best friend in college, Joe, graduated a semester before I did and went to work for an aerospace company located back in my hometown of Kalamazoo, Michigan. It wasn't long after he started working there that I received a letter from him telling me he had given his life to Jesus. Yes, this was back in the 1980s before the internet, cell phones, e-mail, and texting. He told me there was a man at his workplace named Mike who did Bible studies at lunchtime. Joe explained that Mike had shared the gospel with him and had led him to Christ. Joe was very excited and encouraged me to consider surrendering my life to Jesus as well. I can remember actually feeling disappointed that he had made that decision as I continued to embrace the enemy's lie that my life as it was without Jesus was far better than it would be with Him.

OFFER OF A LIFETIME

Three quarters of the way through my last semester in college, I had three job offers: one in Indianapolis, Indiana; one in Findley, Ohio; and one at the same company my best friend was working at in Kalamazoo. God knew exactly where He wanted me. He opened the door wide by making the offer from the company in Kalamazoo 25 percent higher than the other two offers. My decision to take the job offer in Kalamazoo was not based on anything spiritual. It was based solely on the higher starting salary. The job offer was for a new position that was created called a manufacturing management trainee.

As far as I know, I was the one and only person they ever hired in what was then a newly created position. I believe God had that position created and the higher salary that came with it just to get me exactly where He wanted me to be.

Joe worked in the engineering department, and I worked in manufacturing. We really didn't see each other much at work, but as I started spending time with him again on weekends, I could see he was different. He started asking me to attend a Bible study at work that he was attending, and he constantly asked me questions about where I stood in my relationship with Jesus. I had started attending church again once I moved back to Kalamazoo, so my ready answer to his questions was, "I'm going to church."

As my best friend, he knew the truth. He knew I had not surrendered my life to Jesus and that I was still believing the lies from the enemy as I continued living my life for myself.

WORKING ON ME

Not long after I started at this company, I purchased a small two-bedroom home just outside of Kalamazoo. After I purchased the home, Joe told me he had a friend in the engineering department who was looking for a place to live. I ended up renting a room to this friend, whose name is Bill, not knowing that he was a dedicated follower of Jesus since his youth. So, there I was with a roommate and a best friend who were both dedicated followers of Jesus and who both had been working to get me to surrender my life to God.

For a short period of time, I continued to believe I would wait until I was older to make that decision and that, while I was young, I would continue to live my life for myself. God, Joe, and Bill had other plans, though.

SAVED AT A CONCERT

In the fall of 1987, a Christian music concert was coming to an auditorium at the local university. Joe and Bill worked on me for a week to go with them. In a weak moment, I finally relented and agreed just to get them to stop bothering me.

The evening of the concert came, and I went with them. It was at Miller Auditorium. As I sat in the first balcony with Joe and Bill and listened to the worship music and the gospel message that I had heard my mom speak of hundreds of times before, I knew I had been living a lie.

At the end of the evening, an opportunity was given to go to the altar in response to the message presented. I knew I needed to go down to the front as the speaker had encouraged those of us in attendance. It was time to profess that I had surrendered my life to Jesus, but I could not stand up. It felt as if someone were pushing down on my shoulders, holding me in my seat, but there was nobody physically there.

By the time a third and final altar call was made, I was confused and started to sweat, wanting to stand yet feeling unable. Suddenly, the weight lifted off my shoulders, and I rose up, feeling light and unhindered. I felt like I was floating as I walked down to the stage to talk to one of the counselors about my decision.

When we got home that evening, I pelted Bill with questions and listened as he told me about his life's journey with God. I thank God for friends who were willing to partner with and be used by God to have an eternal impact on my life, and I thank Him for praying parents. Today, I know that Joe and Bill as well as others were an answer to years of a mother's prayers for her son.

When I arrived at work on that next Monday, Joe sought me out and told me that Mike, the man who had led him to Christ, wanted to talk to me at lunch.

Later on, when I arrived at Mike's cubical, he smiled and asked me to sit down. He proceeded to tell me that he was sitting ten rows behind me at the concert and that God had placed it on his heart to pray for me. He invited me to attend a weekly lunchtime Bible study in one of the company's conference rooms. He also asked if I would like to do a weekly study in the evening with Joe, Bill, and two other young men from work. I had no idea why I was saying yes, but I did, and I did so immediately!

Of those who attended the evening Bible study, two of us were new believers, two had been believers for most of their lives, and one guy had not yet made a decision for Christ. (He made a decision for Jesus after our first evening gathering.)

Mike started off by teaching us the definition of some of the words we would come across as we read our Bibles. We studied words such as *repentance, grace, mercy, salvation, righteousness, love, redemption,* among others. We looked at what the Bible had to say about dating, marriage, finance, friendship, work, sharing our faith, and what it meant to be a bond servant. He called it *Bible Boot Camp,* but what he was actually doing was discipling us. He encouraged us to read the Proverb of the day for a year. (On the first day of the month, we read Proverbs 1, on the second day of the month Proverbs 2, and so on.) He had us pray out loud, which for some was uncomfortable at first. He also challenged us to memorize Scripture. I still remember the first Scripture verse he had us memorize:

> It is for freedom that Christ has set us free. Stand firm, then, and do not let yourselves be burdened again by a yoke of slavery.
>
> - GALATIANS 5:1

We met weekly for close to a year, studying what the Bible had to say about these and other foundational truths we could apply to our lives as young men. Over time, we added a couple younger men to the group. Though we attended different churches and worked at different companies, we were bound together as brothers in Christ.

As the year came to an end, Mike started talking to us about what God was calling us to do and how we would serve Him. He told us we had a job to do and we needed to pray and seek out God's call on our lives. During this time, Ephesians 2:10 was at the forefront of my mind, especially the words "which he prepared in advance for us to do." I started praying, "God, I know I am your workmanship created in Christ Jesus to do good works that You have prepared in advance for me to do. Father, reveal what those good works are and help me to be effective in walking them out."

The answer I received was not the one I was expecting. I felt Him telling me, "I have you right where I want you. Go into the world I have placed you in and tell people about Me."

I knew then that my calling was not much different than that of other believers—whether they be missionaries serving on foreign fields or ministering in the workplace. I understood from that point on that I was to be used right where I was.

HOW MY WORKPLACE BECAME MY MINISTRY

As my commitment to serve God became stronger, I became more involved in the local church and began attending small groups. I couldn't shake the feeling that God was using the local church as an avenue to build up and train individuals for the purpose of being released into the world each week to make a difference for His Kingdom.

Gathering together on Sundays to sing songs of worship to my Lord and Savior, to be taught about who His Word says He is, and to build relationships with like-minded followers of Jesus encouraged me immensely. There were always opportunities to pray for, encourage, and build each other up as followers of the one true God, but for the most part, everyone I spent time with at church or in small groups had already made a decision for Christ.

I knew the place for me where I could most be effective to partner with God and reach the lost was the very place I spent the majority of my time, week in and week out: my workplace.

As I prayed about what was the best way to conduct a workplace ministry, I felt as though God revealed to me that I was to love my neighbor as myself, be kind, care about those I worked with, and build relationships with them. Then, I believed He would open the doors for conversation and take care of the rest. It seemed far too simple at the time, but this revelation has been foundational for me for decades since in how I approach my workplace ministry.

DOERS OF THE WORD

All along the way, God was teaching me an important lesson on what it meant to apply His principles in my everyday life. It was one thing for me to learn and gain understanding, but it was a totally different thing for me to apply what I had learned or put it into practice.

We can read our Bibles, attend Bible studies, and listen to great sermons, but if we don't put God's Word into practice and apply it to our everyday lives as God tells us in James 1, we can become merely hearers of His Word and not doers: Verses 22–25 read:

> Do not merely listen to the word, and so deceive yourselves. Do what it says. Anyone who listens to the

word but does not do what it says is like someone who looks at his face in a mirror and, after looking at himself, goes away and immediately forgets what he looks like. But whoever looks intently into the perfect law that gives freedom, and continues in it—not forgetting what they have heard, but doing it—they will be blessed in what they do.

SEE A NEED, MEET IT

Not long after the weekly discipleship meetings were completed with Mike, I was approached by Stan, a man who also attended the weekly Bible studies and prayer gatherings we had at work. He shared that he was part of the leadership group of a nonprofit called the Body of Christ (BOC). He explained that it was a group of Christians who had joined together to bring Christian music artists and entertainers to the Kalamazoo area to minister to the lost and brokenhearted. He shared how they were in the midst of the ambitious undertaking of holding a music festival that summer with multiple artists over a weekend at one of the local fairgrounds. Furthermore, he told me that they were in need of extra help.

I decided to get involved.

What I found as I began to serve was a group of believers who saw a need and got together to meet that need. In the late 1980s and early 1990s, Christian music was not as accepted and as big as it is today. As far as contemporary worship went, we were still in the overhead projector phase.

Those participating in BOC did not ask why the church wasn't doing certain things. Instead, they asked, "What can we do?" They felt led by the Holy Spirit to fill this void and over the years brought many artists into the area.

The event I was involved with was held in the summer of 1990 and was called *Mannafest*. It was held at the Allegan County Fairgrounds and featured bands Russia, Margret Becker, Harvest, Kenny Marks, and Mylon Lefevre. Thousands of people attended, and hundreds of them made first-time decisions for Jesus.

My part in all of it, besides prayer, was to be in charge of the food vendors. We had to provide a pavilion area for people to purchase lunch and dinner.

As I contacted businesses in the food industry, explaining what we were doing and why they should be a part of it, the responses were less than encouraging. God used this situation to teach me that just running out and doing things in my own strength would never be as effective as involving Him. I had not covered these meetings with food vendors in prayer prior to speaking with them.

Being a young mid-twenties, type-A personality, I thought I could just go out and make it happen. It's hard to believe that in 1990 not everyone felt a Christian music festival in rural southwest Michigan would draw in enough people to make it worth their while. At a BOC meeting, I expressed frustration at my inability to get food vendors to commit. I received some valuable counseling from a couple of the group leaders about covering this situation with prayer.

After focused prayer and some consistent pestering on my part, we were able to get three food vendors to commit to the event. We had pizza, hamburger and hot dog, and chicken vendors. Not one of the three vendors were prepared for the number of hungry people that showed up to worship the living God. They had to scramble to get extra food brought in to meet the demand. It was a testimony to God's goodness.

At the end of the day, I was checking in with the food vendors, and one of them shared he came expecting this to be a total waste of his day and really had not wanted to be there. He wasn't even sure why he had said yes. He then proceeded to tell me that it was one of the most profitable days they had ever had despite the setback of not being able to keep up with the volume. He was amazed at how kind and courteous most everyone was.

God used that day in a mighty way, not only to change the lives of so many who were in attendance, but also to bless those food vendors who stepped out and said yes to an event they thought would most likely be a waste of their time.

My wife, Karen, was one of the counselors who met with people who made first-time decisions or recommitments to Christ. One of the people she met with and followed up on was a young boy. Years later, she was talking to a friend who told her that same young man went on to be a youth pastor. When we partner with God to have an eternal impact on one life, we have no idea of what His plans are for that person and the number of lives that will be changed based on that one decision. God showed up in a mighty way that day as we worshiped and cried out to Him at a county fairground in the middle of a field.

The BOC was a group of interdenominational people who didn't wait for their local church to tell them to go and do something. They heard from God and were obedient to His call. Their local churches helped to equip them and were at the center of this outreach in many ways, but the members of BOC didn't wait for their pastors to put a plan together and say this is what they needed to go and do.

Too often, we look to our pastors and church leadership to put all the programs and systems in place for outreach. Yes, there are many great outreaches that are associated with church bodies, but we miss out, in many cases, on what God has for us personally to accomplish for His Kingdom. As lovers of God, we can't wait for unbelievers to show up at the front doors of our churches. We must go out. The BOC's *Mannafest* weekend is one of the foundational events that shaped how I see ministry today.

As my time with BOC came to a close, I was in my mid-twenties. Up to this point, God had used three things to shape my view of what partnering with Him in the marketplace is all about:

1. My mom's impacting the lives of those around her;
2. My being part of the discipleship group through work with Mike;
3. My involvement with the BOC and the *Mannafest Christian Music Festival.*

It was a couple years later in the summer of 1992 that the other life-changing event occurred. That, of course, was my last encounter with Dave and what I learned after his death.

[4]
GETTING OUT OF THE BOAT

I STAYED at this company three more years, working hard to be the best employee I could be. During that time, I held three more positions. I stayed involved with Bible studies and prayer in the workplace as well as leading small groups with my wife in our home for our church.

It was also during this time that I prayed and asked God to give me His vision for how He wanted me to approach the marketplace ministry He had called me to. I began to feel a stirring and directional pull toward starting my own business.

When I finally got to a point where I felt this pull to start a business was from God, I sat down with Karen after dinner one evening and explained my feelings to her. Being the amazing wife she is, she just looked at me after we prayed and said, "If you are sure this is where God is calling us, then I am in it with you." I had already done some reading and ran some numbers prior to talking to her, so after getting her yes, I shared that we would need to sell the house we had just built on five acres in the country and move back to town into something smaller and much less expensive. This was a real test for both her and me, as her father and I had built this home with our own hands. He was a retired general contractor, and we worked side by side for nine months building Karen's dream home.

I wish I could say it was easy to let that material possession go, as we knew this was what God was calling us to do, but I would not be telling the truth. There were tears and conversations around doing what He was calling us to do, but each time we came back to knowing we were doing the right thing.

After living and enjoying our new home we had built, we put it up for sale one year after we had moved in. I knew we were being tested. We had made plans to raise our family and grow old together there. My best friend, Joe, and his family lived just down the road from us. We could not have picked a better location for our home. But to be obedient to what we felt God was calling us to, we had to sell it.

We did not let it go easily, though. We decided that we would fleece this out and see if this was truly from God, so we made the asking price twenty thousand dollars higher than what our realtor recommended. She tried to talk us out of it, but we held fast, and she listed the house at the higher number.

You guessed it. The house sold to the first family that looked at it for just under the full asking price.

Karen and I had shared with our realtor what we felt God was calling us to do, but she was still surprised at the results. I think both Karen and I were secretly hoping it wouldn't sell, but neither of us was surprised when it did.

With this sale, we were excited to see what God would have in store for us—what kind of business He would lead us to start and how He would use it and us to have an impact for His Kingdom.

STEPPING ONTO THE WAVES

We sold the home and moved into town. I fully expected it wouldn't be long before I would be resigning from my current job and starting the business that had been laid on my heart. I had been working in manufacturing for six years at this point and had learned a lot about managing and leading people and projects. I had also gained an understanding of foundational principles on becoming salt and light in the workplace, which we will discuss in depth later in a future chapter.

I knew self-education was a key factor for starting and running my own business, so during the evening hours, I submerged myself in books on that subject. My wife and I are avid readers, so at that time, we did not spend money on cable television. Each night after dinner and getting the kids settled into bed, we would read. I not only read books on starting a business, but also on cost accounting, tax laws, leadership, and autobiographies on people who had started successful businesses. These books, along with the

Bible and much prayer, led me to conclude that my business would be a manufacturing business. As I look back on that decision, it seems like common sense since my experience was in manufacturing in the first place, but at the time, I wasn't sure where He was leading me. Besides, Karen and I were open to do whatever He wanted us to do.

Originally, when I was working in manufacturing, I thought God was training me to hold a leadership position in that organization and preparing me to possibly run that company someday. As I look back on that time, I realize God was giving me practical and spiritual training in the workplace, getting Karen and me ready for the future launch of our businesses.

Two years went by before doors began to open and the business was ready to be launched. After we sold our home, I had expected that, within four to six months, we would have a clear vision for what we were to do. Over my thirty-two-year walk with God, I have learned again and again that His ways are not my ways and His timing is not always my timing.

As much as I tried to get out in front of Him over those two years and do something, anything, He would close the doors and make it evident that that was not what He wanted for us. Karen and I had consistently prayed that He would open wide the doors and make evident what He wanted us to do and where He wanted us to be.

STEADYING OUR STEPS

After two years of roadblocks and a couple more promotions, I began to second-guess myself and wonder if I had heard God correctly. It was then, while questioning my hearing, the doors to a manufacturing job shop began to open. Doug, a close friend, was putting up a small, 600-square-foot pole barn, and he offered to rent it to me very inexpensively. Two men with whom I had built relationships and who sold machines offered to help me get financing. I purchased two machines to get started.

My mom and dad offered to make a small loan to us with no payments due until we could afford to make them. This along with our life savings, including cashing in our 401k, would be enough to get us started.

In November of 1995, we officially launched TMD Machining Inc. The two machines we ordered arrived in December, and in January 1996, we were ready to start machining parts for customers. As we prepared for this new venture, I felt strongly that it was not ethical to run a business on the side and stay in my current position. In early January, I went in and spoke with the VP of manufacturing to whom I reported and told him I felt led by God to start a business. I gave him a two-month notice.

After resigning, I imagine many of my coworkers doubted my sanity. "How could anyone leave a secure position?" many of them may have wondered. Starting a new business seemed like a crazy notion. I had a great job with a very good company that helped me manage my family responsibilities. My children were age seven, three, and one, and we had one on the way. Karen was a stay-at-home mom focused on raising our children and pouring into their lives. Leaving my job meant no paycheck or insurance for who knew how long. In the world's economy, this made no sense at all, but we trusted God and His direction.

Between my resignation and the first day as owner of a manufacturing business, it quickly became evident that God's timing was much better than mine. I had no work lined up for the machines as we embarked on this new journey. We prayed and had peace that the work would come.

During the last few weeks at my job, my friend Doug and I went to see an old friend who was working at a local Fortune 500 company. As we shared with our friend the machine shop's start-up and the missing ingredient of actual work to perform, he smiled and said, "Your timing couldn't be better." He went on to tell us that his company was in the process of offloading a major amount of work and their existing suppliers could not handle any more product. They had an immediate need for all the open machine capacity we had! We left the building that day with the back of my family's Roadmaster station wagon filled with raw material and purchase orders for product they needed turned around within days.

Doug started working with me on a part-time basis, and I was no longer praying about where the work would come from. Now, we were praying about how to get it all done! It wasn't long before Doug resigned from his job and was working full-time with me in this new venture.

CALLING OUT TO THE MASTER

A start-up is difficult, and this one was no different. At my previous job, I had an HR department, accounting people, machine programmers, planners, and all the other people I could rely on. With my own business, I had to wear all those hats and run the machines as well.

Additionally, I had always worked more than forty hours a week, working eight-plus hours a day during the week and working most Saturdays as well. During this start-up phase, I allowed my work hours to get out of control. I continued to pray and had a Bible sitting on my desk (which was a sheet of plywood), but I was out of rhythm with reading the Word of God. I felt as though my outreach to others was nonexistent, and this saddened me.

We were bringing in diverse new work, but as a start-up, I was spending money on supplies and materials that were needed at a rapid rate. Not only was I working pretty much nonstop, but we were unable to take a paycheck out of the business.

Nearly six months after leaving my job, I came home from working one evening around 2:00 a.m. Instead of crawling into bed, which my body really wanted to do, I walked into our living room and lay face down on the floor and began to pray. I cried out to God, asking Him if I had heard His voice correctly. Nothing made sense to me at that moment. In extreme exhaustion, I found myself doubting. We were coming very close to totally depleting our savings and having no money to continue financing the business. I was working way too much, trying to survive the rigors of a business launch. I felt as though I was having little to no impact for God's Kingdom through this business when the very reason we started it in the first place was to make an impact.

As I lay there with my face buried in the carpet, peace began to pour over me that I had never felt before and have never felt in the same way since. It was like I was placed inside a capsule and He stripped away all the cares and burdens I was carrying. God let me know I was right where I was supposed to be. He assured me that I had heard His voice. His assurance and peace were overwhelming. I did not want to get up and leave that hiding place. It seemed that I had only been lying there a few minutes, but it had actually been over an hour that God graced me with His presence in this way.

READJUSTING AND FIXING MY EYES ON JESUS

I wish I could say I got up the next morning and everything was perfect, but the fact of the matter was the circumstances I was dealing with were the same. What changed was my perspective. I knew without any doubt, as I got up and went to work that morning, that God had called me to this and He would provide what was needed. I also came to the realization that I was trying to do too much and to do it in my own strength. I began to get back into reading His Word consistently, continued to pray, and returned to seeking opportunities to be salt and light.

After seven months without a paycheck and our savings depleted, we were finally able to start taking a paycheck from the company. Shortly before we were able to receive our first paycheck, however, a friend we attended church with asked if we would be willing to give an offering that would go toward a Mexican vacation for our pastor and his wife. He had arranged an opportunity for them to travel with him and his wife for a much-needed break, but finances were an obstacle for our pastor and his wife.

Karen and I discussed this opportunity to give to our pastor's time off and prayed about it together. In the end, we both felt that, even though we had limited funds, God was calling us to give from our lack and trust Him. I was drawn to 1 Kings 17, which is the story of Elijah and the widow at Zarephath:

> Some time later the brook dried up because there had been no rain in the land. Then the word of the Lord came to him: "Go at once to Zarephath in the region of Sidon and stay there. I have directed a widow there to supply you with food." So he went to Zarephath. When he came to the town gate, a widow was there gathering sticks. He called to her and asked, "Would you bring me a little water in a jar so I may have a drink?" As she was going to get it, he called, "And bring me, please, a piece of

bread." "As surely as the Lord your God lives," she replied, "I don't have any bread—only a handful of flour in a jar and a little olive oil in a jug. I am gathering a few sticks to take home and make a meal for myself and my son, that we may eat it—and die." Elijah said to her, "Don't be afraid. Go home and do as you have said. But first make a small loaf of bread for me from what you have and bring it to me, and then make something for yourself and your son. For this is what the Lord, the God of Israel, says: 'The jar of flour will not be used up and the jug of oil will not run dry until the day the Lord sends rain on the land.'" She went away and did as Elijah had told her. So there was food every day for Elijah and for the woman and her family. For the jar of flour was not used up and the jug of oil did not run dry, in keeping with the word of the Lord spoken by Elijah.

- VV. 7-16

This passage helped to solidify what I felt God was telling us. He was affirming He would supply what we needed and our funds would not run out. This was no different from how the widow's jars of flour and oil did not go empty. However, as the request was made to give the money, I did not feel as though I was gathering sticks to prepare a meal for my family so that we could eat it and die like the widow. At the same time, I did think it was a fiscally crazy thing to be doing. Yet, we gave, and our money never ran out. The jar got pretty empty, but we had enough to live on until we were able to take our first paycheck.

As is true for a lot of start-ups, finances were very tight, and unexpected purchases still had to be made. For quite some time, vacations were a luxury we could not afford. This is the part of the story where God gets all the glory.

After about three years of being in business, Karen's mom and dad invited us and her brother and his wife on a trip to Mexico, all expenses paid. My mom and dad offered to watch the kids for the week, so we quickly agreed. This happened a few more times over the years.

On our fifth trip to Mexico, we were sitting on our balcony, praying and enjoying God's creation when He brought to our minds the gift we had given the pastor all those years before. I don't know why I hadn't put it all together prior to that, but as Karen and I sat in His presence, I felt God reminding me of that gift and how He had repaid us many times over for our obedience.

Karen and I did not give expecting anything in return. We gave because we felt it was a privilege and all that we had that was good was a gift from God.

My parents taught me the principle of tithing and budgeting early on in my life. In most cases, you do not get five of the exact same gifts in return for what you gave like we did with the trips to Mexico. I am a firm believer in setting aside the first fruits and giving tithes and offerings to God, knowing He is the Creator of the universe and He loves us and cares about our needs. Malachi 3:10 says,

"Bring the whole tithe into the storehouse, that there may be food in my house. Test me in this," says the Lord Almighty, "and see if I will not throw open the floodgates of heaven and pour out so much blessing that there will not be room enough to store it."

ROCK AND REFUGE

In 1997, we moved our business to 3.5 acres and built a new 10,000-square-foot building in Plainwell, Michigan. After selling the home my father-in-law and I had built, it was a blessing to work with him again on our new building. His general contracting background and connections made the construction of the building go smoothly. He enjoyed being a part of the team.

Over the next twenty-plus years, we have grown every year but one—the year we did not expand was by choice. We felt led to slow down and put the necessary systems in place to handle more growth. We now have three businesses and eleven acres in our industrial park, with three buildings that will total 150,000 square feet when our next planned addition is completed.

When we moved in 1997, we had seven employees. Twenty-two years later, we are closing in on two hundred.

In 2008, as the nation dealt with an economic slowdown, we continued to grow our business. I do not say any of this to take credit for the successes. All glory and honor for any of the accomplishments of these businesses belong to God as He provided the vision for starting them and has provided all that has been needed for them to prosper. By no means, am I saying everything has been easy and we have been perfect in all our decisions. During this journey, we have been on the mountaintops, as well as in the valleys, but through it all God has been our rock and refuge.

> Yes, my soul, find rest in God; my hope comes from him. Truly he is my rock and my salvation; he is my fortress, I will not be shaken. My salvation and my honor depend on God; he is my mighty rock, my refuge.
>
> - PSALM 62:5-7

A GOD-FIRST WORKPLACE

From early on in the business, daily Bible reading and prayer have been going on at break time. We have employees who gather on their breaks and read a chapter out of Proverbs or a psalm and pray.

Each Wednesday at lunch, I gather for prayer and study with some family members and a couple of men I knew before I started the businesses—men whom God has seen fit to call to be a part of His work inside my companies. Inside this group is family representing four generations—my grandmother, at ninety-seven years of age; my mother; my wife; and me, as well as representation from my children who are all grown and working in the businesses.

Over the decades, we have watched God move in the marketplace, breaking bondages, healing physical ailments, and changing lives for eternity.

WALKING ON WATER

Leaving my job and becoming a business owner was both Karen's and my getting-out-of-the-boat-and-walking-on-water moment. It was much like what Peter experienced. In Matthew 14:25–29, we read:

> Shortly before dawn Jesus went out to them, walking on the lake. When the disciples saw him walking on the lake, they were terrified. "It's a ghost," they said, and cried out in fear. But Jesus immediately said to them: "Take courage! It is I. Don't be afraid." "Lord, if it's you," Peter replied, "tell me to come to you on the water." "Come," he said. Then Peter got down out of the boat, walked on the water and came toward Jesus.

Over the years, as I have counseled with people making their big, sometimes risky, decisions that don't always make sense from the world's viewpoint, I have used the words from this passage often. I have encouraged them by saying that sometimes they just have to be willing to trust God and get out of the boat.

Early on as I thought about starting a company, I felt God speaking to me, saying, "Tom, read the passage." Then, as I read the passage over and over, this thought struck me: It's not just that Peter got out of the boat, but it's also that Jesus told him to come and *then* Peter got out of the boat.

Karen and I had prayed through and were convinced of what Jesus had called us to before we made the decision to get out of the boat. When I am talking with someone about their get-out-of-the-boat moment, I'm always quick to caution, "Make sure God is calling you before you get out of the boat."

I also encourage people to make sure their plans line up with Scripture. When you are considering walking on water in a storm, you want to make sure God is calling you to do that, so you can remain focused on Him.

I believe these get-out-of-the-boat moments and the hearing-God's-calling-before-moving-forward moments are in most cases large, life-changing events. I am not talking about becoming paralyzed with inactivity because we are waiting to hear from God about everyday decisions. He has given us the Scriptures and His Holy Spirit to give us direction on how He wants us to go about serving Him and walking out our daily lives. So, access them when you need to know what to do. Psalm 119:105 says it best: "Your word is a lamp for my feet, a light on my path."

In the coming chapters, we will walk through some of the specifics on how God has worked and moved in our marketplace mission field. I am sure you have similar stories and experiences. Hopefully, this will help to further your walk as a marketplace missionary.

[5]
HAS GOD CALLED US TO THE MARKETPLACE?

In the fall of 2018, the Barna Group did a study of employed Christians who agree somewhat or strongly that their faith is very important in their lives today. These were full-time, part-time, or self-employed Christians and included those who were unpaid workers of a family business. What they found in this study was that, while 82 percent of those interviewed felt Christians should act ethically in the workplace and 66 percent felt Christians should make friends with non-Christians, only 24 percent said sharing the gospel in the workplace is a Christian's responsibility.[1]

Additionally, the people surveyed included those who attended church regularly (defined as two times per month) and who also believed the Bible is God's written Word. Using this criterion, less than 20 percent of the US population attend church regularly and believe the Bible is God's Word. The percentage is even smaller if you compare it to the global population. Then, when you take the 24 percent of those surveyed who believe that sharing the gospel in the workplace is a Christian's responsibility and compare it to the entire US population, you end up with less than 4 percent of the US population believing that sharing the gospel in the workplace is a Christian's responsibility. My experiences over a thirty-plus-year career would lead me to believe that number is accurate if not a little high.

If we were to examine how many Christians were praying about and actively pursuing opportunities to share the gospel in the marketplace, the number would most likely be even smaller. I am not sharing these numbers to condemn us. I am sharing them to give us a perspective on where we stand today in the US with taking the gospel into the workplace.

If a major portion of the regular churchgoing population does not believe sharing the gospel in the workplace is something we should do, why don't they? What does God's Word tell us about this? What kind of examples did Jesus give us through His actions?

Let's start with the question of why most people don't believe it is their responsibility.

WHAT'S OUR PART?

In large part, our American church has evolved into seeker-friendly gatherings. We have been deceived by the enemy that all we need to do is invite people to our churches and let the pastors and church staff take it from there. But this is not what Jesus commanded us to do in the Great Commission. (See Matthew 28:18–20.) He did not command us to go into all the nations and invite the lost to church, although this is good and something we should do. But it's only a start. What Jesus actually commanded each of us to do is to go and make disciples of all nations by proclaiming the truth about Him.

People tell me all the time that, yes, they believe we're called to make disciples of all the nations, but they also believe we can do that apart from sharing our faith in the workplace. They believe the Great Commission applies only to sending missionaries to other countries. There's a big issue with this mindset. The verse says, "all the nations," which applies to the one we are currently living in. If less than 20 percent of Americans attend church two times or more per month, and many don't attend at all, no matter how seeker friendly we make the local church, it will not have the desired impact because people just aren't attending. We need to *go* and actively be about our Father's business. We must not sit and wait for the lost to come walking through the front doors of our churches.

The truth is most of us in the marketplace spend a large part of our lifetime working and building relationships with those with whom we work. If we have committed our whole lives to God, we cannot treat Him like the vehicle we drive to work every day—when we get to work, we turn Him off and leave Him in the parking lot. If we are willing to go to the marketplace and do our best to live according to His principles but are unwilling to share our story and take opportunities to share our faith, then we are making a choice to limit how we can be used by God in fulfilling the Great Commission.

We all have been given free will—the freedom to choose how we will engage with God. That freedom is not only granted in our decision to accept His free gift of salvation. We retain that freedom even after we become His followers and whether or not we will obey what He teaches through His Word and the promptings of the Holy Spirit who has been deposited in us. The whole of it is that, once we become followers of Jesus, we are in effect choosing each day how much of our lives we are willing to surrender to Him. As we read His Word, there is no doubt that He wants us to surrender our entire lives over to Him, which includes the lives we live in the marketplace. Mark 8:34 tells us,

> Then he called the crowd to him along with his disciples and said: "Whoever wants to be my disciple must deny themselves and take up their cross and follow me."

No differently than Adam and Eve who had the freedom to choose if they would eat from the Tree of the Knowledge of Good and Evil, we choose each day if we are going to eat from the fruit of this world or take up our cross and surrender all to Jesus.

As His followers, if we are going to do our part in working to help fulfill the Great Commission, we have to recognize the workplace as an important mission field. We can't only represent Him by being the excellent employees He calls us to be. We must also be prepared and ready to share His message of salvation with those with whom we're working. This obedience makes us different, and our lights will shine brightly in the darkness.

As we wrestle with society's view on God's presence in the workplace, schools, and other public places, I believe we need to change our perspective on how we view His presence in these places.

I had a conversation not long ago with a fellow believer on the removal of the Ten Commandments from the walls of some schools and the removal of the prayer prior to commencement. This fellow Christian made the statement that it is no wonder we are dealing with certain struggles in our schools. He said what else could we expect as we are removing God from our schools.

Now, I will admit I would love it if we could continue to thank God, pray at school functions, and have the Ten Commandments listed on the walls, but the removal of those things is not removing God from the schools. Despite what some of us think, the governments of this world are not more powerful than the Creator of the heavens and the earth. He is the One whom we serve. As His sons and daughters, we represent Him as His ambassadors, and unless we choose to check Him at the door, we are taking God with us into these places and have the opportunity to partner with Him as the Holy Spirit leads us.

In some countries, you could be thrown in prison and even killed if you profess faith in Christ. For those who face this threat every day, their governments' efforts to eradicate Christianity in their countries are driving the fire of evangelism. Many have thriving house churches with some of the fastest-growing bodies of believers on the globe.

> God was reconciling the world to himself in Christ, not counting people's sins against them. And he has committed to us the message of reconciliation. We are therefore Christ's ambassadors, as though God were making His appeal through us.
>
> - 2 CORINTHIANS 5:19-20

In writing to the Corinthian church, the apostle Paul referred to Christians as *ambassadors*. An ambassador is a minister or diplomatic representative; more specifically, *Merriam-Webster's Collegiate Dictionary, Eleventh Edition* defines an ambassador as "a diplomatic agent of the highest rank accredited to a foreign government or sovereign as the resident representative of his or her own government or sovereign."

Then, in 1 Peter 2:11, we are called "aliens and foreigners in this world" (TPT). When we make the decision to repent and surrender our lives to God, from a heavenly perspective, our citizenship changes. We are no longer spiritual citizens of this world. Instead, we've become citizens of the Kingdom of God.

We must now come to understand what our new citizenship means concerning how we live our lives and what priorities our citizenship sets for our everyday experiences. As I have already mentioned, for many of us, a big portion of our lives is spent in the marketplace. So, as we consider our Kingdom citizenship and our calling by God, what conclusions can we draw about how we engage with others in the marketplace based on how Jesus, our example, approached the opportunities He had with people in His everyday life on Earth?

JESUS AND THE GREAT COMMISSION

One of the clearest examples of Jesus sharing the good news and teaching in the marketplace shows up in the moments surrounding calling His first disciples.

> One day as Jesus was standing by the Lake of Gennesaret, the people were crowding around him and listening to the word of God. He saw at the water's edge two boats, left there by the fishermen, who were washing their nets. He got into one of the boats, the one belonging to Simon, and asked him to put out a little from shore. Then he sat down and taught the people from the boat. When he had finished speaking, he said to Simon, "Put out into deep water, and let down the nets for a catch." Simon

answered, "Master, we've worked hard all night and haven't caught anything. But because you say so, I will let down the nets." When they had done so, they caught such a large number of fish that their nets began to break. So they signaled their partners in the other boat to come and help them, and they came and filled both boats so full that they began to sink. When Simon Peter saw this, he fell at Jesus' knees and said, "Go away from me, Lord; I am a sinful man!" For he and all his companions were astonished at the catch of fish they had taken, and so were James and John, the sons of Zebedee, Simon's partners.

- LUKE 5:1-10

Jesus walked right into Peter's and James's place of business as they were finishing their workday and cleaning up before going home. The workplace was the Lake of Gennesaret also known as the Sea of Galilee. By this time, Jesus had begun His ministry, and they were well aware of who He was. They had met Him and spent time with Him. (See John 1:35–42.) Sometime after meeting them, Jesus came to where Peter, James, and John worked and taught the crowd from a piece of their equipment (their boat). After He finished, He performed a miracle in that marketplace.

In other places in God's Word, we see Jesus teaching in the countryside, homes, towns, synagogues, and yes, also in the marketplace. To be of the mindset that we are going to pick and choose what venues God can use us to share the good news does not follow Jesus' example.

Now, it would probably not be wise to stand on a machine in the middle of our workplaces and start preaching at people, but we can partner with God to have the largest possible impact for His Kingdom. Our focus should not be on where and how we will do this. We must be open to how God wants to use us to share the good news, and yes, we must honor those we work for by being excellent at doing the work they are paying us to do. In a later chapter, we will discuss some ideas on how to balance sharing our faith with excelling at our craft.

BE ABOUT THE BUSINESS OF SHARING THE GOSPEL

The apostle Paul, who is credited with writing nearly two thirds of the New Testament, worked with Aquila and Priscilla as a tentmaker.

> When Paul left Athens he traveled to Corinth, where he met a Jewish man named Aquila, who was originally from northeast Turkey. He and his wife, Priscilla, had recently immigrated from Italy to Corinth because Emperor Claudius had expelled all the Jews from Rome. Since Paul and Aquila were both tentmakers by trade, Paul moved in with them and they became business partners.
>
> - ACTS 18:1-3, TPT

As we read through Paul's writings in the New Testament, there is no doubt that he was not just working alongside Aquila and Priscilla in the marketplace and living with them. He was also sharing the good news with everyone he met. He gave personal greetings to Aquila and Priscilla in Romans 16:3–4; 1 Corinthians 16:19; and 2 Timothy 4:19. They were also helpful to Apollos in his ministry (Acts 18:26). Working in the tentmaking business, Aquila, Pricilla, and Paul were marketplace missionaries doing God's work in their business and in their home.

The enemy wants to render us ineffective by leading us to believe that it is inappropriate to share the good news in the marketplace. Once we have made a decision to repent and give our lives over to Jesus, the devil does not want us sharing what we know as followers of Jesus. Satan knows we are citizens of heaven, but as much as we will allow him to, he wants to distract us from God's purposes and plans for our lives.

We are not left here as God's children to kick back and receive all the blessings that are associated with becoming part of His family. Yes, there are many great promises and blessings associated with being His children, but we are called to be about the business of sharing the gospel.

For I am not ashamed of the gospel, because it is the power of God that brings salvation to everyone who believes: first to the Jew, then to the Gentile. For in the gospel the righteousness of God is revealed—a righteousness that is by faith from first to last, just as it is written: "The righteous will live by faith."

- ROMANS 1:16-17

So then, if we are not ashamed of the gospel and we are called to share it, not just in our local churches, but also in the marketplace, how do we effectively do that?

Over the next few chapters, I will discuss some principles I have seen work over the past few decades. Just remember while reading this that, if we become religious about doing things in one certain way and are not listening for God's direction, our outreach can become about a process or way of doing things instead of about our relationship with God and who He is.

---

1. "What Faith Looks Like in the Workplace," *Barna*, October 30, 2018, https://www.barna.com/research/faith-workplace/.

[6]

PRAYER IN THE MARKETPLACE

As WE EMBARK on sharing our faith in the marketplace, it is important to remember we are going into a battle in which we are not fighting against people but against the enemy and his schemes. Ephesians 6:11–18 says:

> Put on the full armor of God, so that you can take your stand against the devil's schemes. For our struggle is not against flesh and blood, but against the rulers, against the authorities, against the powers of this dark world and against the spiritual forces of evil in the heavenly realms. Therefore put on the full armor of God, so that when the day of evil comes, you may be able to stand your ground, and after you have done everything, to stand. Stand firm then, with the belt of truth buckled around your waist, with the breastplate of righteousness in place, and with your feet fitted with the readiness that comes from the gospel of peace. In addition to all this, take up the shield of faith, with which you can

extinguish all the flaming arrows of the evil one. Take the helmet of salvation and the sword of the Spirit, which is the word of God. And pray in the Spirit on all occasions with all kinds of prayers and requests. With this in mind, be alert and always keep on praying for all the Lord's people.

The workplace can be a spiritually dark place, and we must realize that, as we let God's light shine through us, we will meet resistance from the enemy. We must take to heart the words from this passage and put on the full armor of God each day as we go to do spiritual battle for His Kingdom. Paul tells us this for our protection and to increase our effectiveness. We would not send out a front-line soldier in our army to do battle in flip flops, shorts, a T-shirt, and a squirt gun. We would send him out fully equipped with the best possible armor and weapons.

In the same way, God wants us to go out with His full armor. These are not items we can obtain in our own strength. We obtain them as followers of Jesus when we put on the mantle of Christ. As we don this spiritual armor, it is not our goal then to go out and pick a fight directly with Satan or his demons. The armor is our protection. It allows us to stand our ground as we go out into the world, share the gospel, and make disciples.

Verse 11 of the above passage tells us to "put on the full armor" so we can take our stand against the devil's schemes. Verse 13 says to "put on the full armor of God" so that, when the day of evil comes, we will be able to stand our ground. For armor to be effective, a soldier needs to understand his armor—how to put it on and how it works. There are many good teachings and commentaries on the armor of God, and if you have not had a chance to study it, I suggest you take some time to do so. Memorizing the armor of God and putting it on through prayer on a daily basis is something I have done and would encourage you to do as well.

A FOUNDATION OF PRAYER

In Ephesians 6:18, Paul tells us to pray in the Spirit on all occasions. As Karen and I embarked on the journey of starting our first company, we covered it in prayer. We prayed and believed for customers we did not yet have as well as employees we had not yet hired. But above everything, we prayed for God's vision for the company and how He wanted to use it. We felt Him calling us to start the business, and we were confident that, if we cried out to Him in prayer, He would give us His direction and make level paths for our feet.

Prayer is critical if we want to have any success in reaching people in the marketplace. A marketplace outreach must be first bathed in prayer. We would not consider sending a missionary to a foreign country without covering them in prayer. The reality is we are all foreigners right where we are (Philippians 3:20), and we should approach prayer for our outreach no differently than we would for the missionary going to another country.

Early on in the business, I started meeting with a former coworker who had come to work with me at my company. As I mentioned in our story a few chapters back, our Wednesday lunch prayer time with family and three key men from leadership within the company has been crucial to the success of our businesses and also our relationships with employees. Joining together to lift up to God the Father business issues, family concerns, and community items has been powerful. Answered prayer and watching God move on the behalf of others, as well as our own, have been constant encouragements. In our businesses, we have fasted and prayed together and have seen God do miracles and move in wonderful ways. We have prayed and have seen physical healings, bondages broken, marriages healed, and people led to a saving relationship with Jesus.

Prayer is foundational in a successful marketplace outreach. Jesus does not say *if* we pray in Matthew 6 but says *when* we pray, letting us know that it is an expectation that we *will* pray. Prayer strengthens our relationship with our Father in heaven, giving us a confidence and peace that transcends all understanding.

> Do not be anxious about anything, but in every situation, by prayer and petition, with thanksgiving, present your requests to God. And the peace of God, which

transcends all understanding, will guard your hearts and your minds in Christ Jesus.

- PHILIPPIANS 4:6-7

UNITE AND CONQUER

Another important principle is finding other followers of Jesus to meet with and specifically pray for your business or career, the people you work with, and each other.

> Two are better than one, because they have a good return for their labor. If either of them falls down, one can help the other up. But pity anyone who falls and has no one to help them up.

- ECCLESIASTES 4:9-10

Jesus sent out the seventy-two, two by two, into the towns ahead of Him:

> After this the Lord appointed the seventy-two others and sent them two by two ahead of him to every town and place where he was about to go. He told them, "The harvest is plentiful, but the workers are few. Ask the Lord of the harvest, therefore, to send out workers into His harvest field."

- LUKE 10:1-2

Finding at least one other believer to pray with and partner with for your marketplace outreach is a biblical principle. At times, as I have discussed this with people, some have interjected to say that they don't work with anyone at their church. Many of the core group of Jesus followers I pray with in the marketplace attend different local churches than the church I attend. We don't always agree on everything we discuss, but we do agree on the foundational issues of the Trinity, the Bible being God's Word, and the only way to spend eternity with our Father in heaven is through a saving relationship with Jesus. There are many denominations who believe the above foundational principles but differ, in some degree, on interpretation of different scriptures.

In the end, despite the differing opinions on Scripture interpretation, I don't believe God is interested in what denomination we are part of. We are either followers of Jesus, or we are not. There are no denominations when it comes to this guiding principle. Pray that God will bring to mind someone to pray with in the marketplace and that the Lord of the harvest would send workers out into the marketplace to work alongside you.

GET PERMISSION

As you begin making plans to meet and pray weekly as a group at your workplace, you should always talk to your leadership or human resource department. They should be aware of what you are intending to accomplish.

One time, an individual who worked for one of our customers visited our facility to do some training. He noticed the stack of Bibles in the corner of our conference room. At one of our breaks, he pulled me aside and asked what the Bibles were for. I told him about the Bible studies we held as well as the prayer that went on at the company. He asked me if he could talk to me more about this after the day was over because he had been feeling the Holy Spirit urging him to do something at his place of employment.

After we finished for the day, he and I sat in my office and talked about his marketplace as a mission field, and I prayed for him and his company. I advised him to inform his human resource department about his plans. I told him that it is always better to be upfront and honest with your leadership about your plans. Even though he had planned to have prayer and Bible study on his own time—at lunchtime or during a break—he would be using his employer's facilities. They should be made aware, I told him. He was a little hesitant but agreed that it was the right avenue to take.

About two weeks later, he called me with exciting news. He did indeed contact his human resource department, and they agreed to allow him to hold a Bible study and prayer time in their conference room once a week at lunch. He was told they would first have to ask the general manager of that facility. He told me that he was invited to meet with the general manager in his office the next day. As he arrived for the meeting, he did not know what to expect and was a little apprehensive. He said the general manager proceeded to tell him that he had been told they wanted to meet and pray prior to work. The general manager told him that, if they were going to pray for the company and the people that worked there, and they were doing this on their time before work, they could use the executive conference room. Obviously, everyone who asks is not told they can use the executive conference room to meet and pray. What a blessing for this new marketplace missionary!

I have met and prayed with men at restaurants or coffee shops prior to work, in homes after work, and in the workplace. There is no one special place to meet and pray. We just need to find a place that works and do it.

As you begin to gather to pray, make sure you establish that you are praying for your marketplace and those who are working there with you. You always want to listen for the Holy Spirit and let Him lead, but if there is no understanding that you and those you have gathered are approaching the marketplace as a mission field, the prayer time can become disjointed and less effective.

WHAT TO PRAY AND HOW TO PRAY IT

I will give you some of the things we pray for on a consistent basis, but I also want to encourage you that prayer is not simply a laundry list of things we take to God and ask Him to do for us. We need to spend some quiet time with Him, listening for what the Holy Spirit wants to communicate to us. The communication must be two ways so we hear from God and our relationship with Him is strengthened. This will help us gain a better understanding of how He wants us to go about His business. Luke 5:16 says this: "Jesus often withdrew to lonely places and prayed."

1. START WITH PRAISE

We often start prayer times at my company with praise and thanksgiving. We all have things to be thankful for even as it pertains to our workplace. In Psalm 100:4, God gives us direction on how He wants us to come into His presence. Thank Him for:

- The job He has provided for you
- The people He has placed around you
- The outreach opportunities He is giving you
- The ability He has given you to excel at your work
- The customers He brings to your company
- The believers He has placed alongside you or is going to place in your path as you do His work
- The answers to prayers He has provided

These are just a few things we can be thankful for at our workplace.

2. PRAY FOR THE LEADERSHIP AT YOUR COMPANY

I do not see any verses in the Bible about sitting around in the break room and grumbling about the leadership in your company, but I do see verses on praying for the leadership.

> I urge you, then, first of all, that petitions, prayers, intercession and thanksgiving be made for all people—for kings and all those in authority, that we may live peaceful and quiet lives in all godliness and holiness.
>
> - 1 TIMOTHY 2:1-2

If we want to see change in our workplaces, cities, and countries, we need to spend less time complaining about the leadership and more time praying for them.

3. PRAY SPECIFICALLY FOR PEOPLE WHO ARE SICK OR DEALING WITH OTHER ISSUES IN THEIR LIVES

If someone brings up an issue to you during the week, let them know you are meeting weekly with others and praying for the company and those in it. Ask if they would like you to pray for their issue. Be sensitive to their privacy. They may be sharing their issue with you but may not want it shared with others. If that is the case, or you just feel led by the Holy Spirit to pray then, ask them if you can pray for them. If you are able to pray for them in private, right then, and they are comfortable with it, then do it. If not, let them know you will be praying for them. Check back with them periodically to see how they're doing.

I have an office, so it is easy for me to close my door and pray for someone in private. On rare occasions, I will pray for someone out on our factory floor. I only do this with someone I know is a follower of Jesus and they have opened up to me about a specific issue in their life. I will be there for them on the spot, if necessary, when they ask me to pray for them.

When people find out you're holding prayer on a specific day, you will find more than a few bumping into you throughout the day, sharing their concerns, and asking for prayer. This can be a powerful part of your marketplace outreach when it is handled correctly.

4. MAKE A LIST OF THE PEOPLE YOU WORK WITH AND PRAY OVER EACH PERSON ON THAT LIST

Pray for the believers in your workplace who are on the list you've made. Pray that their relationship with their heavenly Father would be strengthened. Pray also for the lost in your workplace that they would recognize they are in need of a savior.

Pray that God would provide divine appointments with those in need of a saving relationship with Him and that He would give you the boldness required and words to share when those opportunities arise.

5. PRAY FOR GOD'S BLESSINGS AND FAVOR

When we pray, God hears us and answers (Jeremiah 29:12–13; 33:3; Psalm 66:17–20; John 9:31; 1 Peter 3:12; 1 John 5:15). Where there is praise and recognition of who He is in any situation, God makes His presence known through blessings, favor, miracles, and provision (Psalm 22:3).

When you pray, pray that He would reign down on your company and those who work there so that your efforts will bring glory to His name.

6. CLAIM THAT THE BUILDINGS AND PROPERTY ARE POSITIONED ON HOLY GROUND

Pray that your company will be used by God for His purposes. Pray that His Kingdom come and His will be done at your company as it is in heaven and that His fiery hedge of protection would surround the facility and those who work there.

7. PRAY THAT GOD WILL USE THE OUTREACH INSIDE THE COMPANY AND EXPAND IT

When God starts something, though it may start small, He is always about expansion and multiplication. Though you may be starting with a few, do not despise the day of small beginnings. Pray that God would increase and multiply your efforts. Pray that your spiritual effort produces much fruit and that what you've begun inside the four walls of your company reaches out into the surrounding neighborhoods and communities.

These are just a few suggestions to help you get started praying for your company and those with whom you work. The more you do this, the more Holy Spirit will lead. Don't get weary in well doing; continue to cry out to your Father in heaven and listen quietly for His answers. He will direct your paths.

Before giving a few examples of how prayer has had an impact at our business, I will finish with this on prayer. I do not believe you can have an effective outreach in the marketplace if it is not built on prayer. Our relationship with God can never be all He wants it to be without our having a strong prayer life. This is a natural and spiritual principle: We can't be in a good relationship with someone if all we do is present them with a to-do list every day. If I woke up each morning and gave Karen a list of tasks that must be accomplished by the end of the day and that was the extent of our conversation, I don't think our relationship would be a good one. (Just as a side note, I do not get up in the morning and give Karen a list of tasks to complete. If I did, I am pretty sure it would not go well for me.)

The same holds true for our prayer life with God. Talk to Him, share your hurts, your desires, and your questions. Converse with Him throughout the day. Let Him know how much you love Him. Don't just say the words, show Him.

Share with Him areas in which you are struggling, and ask Him to forgive you for any areas you are missing the best He has for you. Tell Him you feel too weak to handle things in certain areas of your life on your own and let Him know you need His help.

Become vulnerable. The Creator of the universe loves you and desires relationship with you. He wants to partner with you in expanding His Kingdom.

Psalm 115:16 says, "The highest heavens belong to the Lord, but the earth he has given to mankind." God is the ruler over all things, but He has given us responsibilities in His creation as His followers. He will give us everything we need to be successful in carrying out our responsibilities as followers of Jesus. A critical component to receiving the wisdom required to accomplish these tasks is prayer. The veil was torn some two thousand years ago, giving us access, through prayer, to the throne room of heaven.

Having therefore, brethren, boldness to enter into the holiest by the blood of Jesus, by a new and living way, which he hath consecrated for us, through the veil, that is to say, his flesh.

- HEBREWS 10:19-20, KJV

For through him we both have access to the Father by one Spirit.

- EPHESIANS 2:18

In him and through faith in him we may approach God
with freedom and confidence.

- EPHESIANS 3:12

HOW PRAYER BROUGHT HEAVEN TO EARTH IN OUR BUSINESS

As previously mentioned, we have some form of corporate
prayer happening each day inside our facility, but along
with that are many Holy Spirit-spontaneous situations or
divine appointments that arise.

A DIVINE APPOINTMENT

One day, in passing, I met someone who had heard about
our manufacturing business and wanted to know if he
could schedule a meeting. He wanted to discuss some
work he was considering us to complete for him. We met
at our facility about a week later, but the work he needed
done was not a good fit for our company. Still, I made
small talk, trying to get to know him a little better.

When I asked him if he had any children, he was
quick to share about his family. He got choked up when he
told me about some of the struggles he was having with
one of his sons. I asked a few questions but, for the most
part, let him share what he was dealing with.

Toward the end of our meeting, I felt led, as I often do,
to ask if he would like prayer for his son. He agreed. I
prayed for him, and he felt God lifting the burden for his

son off him and peace descending on him. He had not experienced peace like that for his son in a long time.

When I finished praying, he looked up with a large smile on his face and told me that he almost didn't come that day. He had done a little research on our company and knew before he came that their work was not a good fit for us. For some reason, he felt he needed to meet with me, so he didn't cancel.

Opportunities like this will happen all the time if we pay attention and are willing to be bold. There are times when people refuse prayer. That's OK. We're only responsible to God for partnering with Him and doing our part. They are responsible for doing theirs.

AN ENCOURAGING WORD

I walk through our shop multiple times each day to see how things are going and talk to employees. This is something I have done since I was a young man. I've always wanted to know more about the people I work with and their families—more than just the picture of them I see at work. This particular day, I was walking through the shop, and I felt the Lord impress me to stop and talk to a specific individual. I was on a mission trying to get something done. So being the knucklehead I can be at times, I ignored the nudge and went about my business.

Returning to my office and taking the same path back, I felt the same nudge again, but again, I ignored it. I started to feel very uncomfortable. I prayed a quick prayer, apologized to God, and asked Him to give me the words He wanted to say to this individual. I had no specifics on what I was going to say, but God created another opportunity for me to obey Him.

As I stood in front of the man to whom God wanted me to speak, I told him that I felt God wanted me to tell him how much God loved him and how God was there for him. The man thanked me, and that was it. I walked away feeling at peace. I had done what I was asked to do.

The next morning, the man arrived at my office door and asked if he could speak to me. He closed the door and sat down. As soon as he began to share, he started to cry. He said that he had been having problems at home and with other relationships as well. He let me know that he had been previously addicted to drugs, and before I had stopped to deliver God's message, he had decided to use again. Because of all his troubles, he was having difficulty coping, and contacting his old dealer was on the forefront of his mind. Though he had been clean for over a year and was attending church, he just felt like he was at the end of his rope and could not handle any more of what he had been facing. The effect those simple but loving words from God had on him stopped him from traveling down a very dark path.

HEALED AT WORK

Our daughter Adrien had been struggling with headaches since high school. By her senior year, they had gotten to the point of making her sick. We took her to our family doctor. He examined her and suggested we take her for an MRI.

A few days after the MRI, I received a call from our physician informing me they saw something on the MRI. "Don't wait," he said. "Pull her out of school and take her to the hospital so she can get a CAT scan. Once this is accomplished, you need to meet with a brain surgeon/doctor to get some answers."

Needless to say, this is not a call you want to receive as a parent. I immediately began to pray as I left work to pick her up. I contacted my wife on the way so she could meet us there.

When we arrived at the hospital, the nurses took her in to help her get prepped for the CAT scan. Other staff ushered us into the waiting room. We waited for what seemed like days, but it was only an hour before we were called into an office to talk to the doctor. He showed us the scan of Adrien's brain and the very visible dark spot on it. He said he did not know what the spot was, but he was fairly confident it was causing her headaches. He felt it would be wise to do a brain catheter, which is a long thin tube that is inserted into an artery in the groin. Through the tube, a special dye is injected into the blood vessels that lead to the brain. This dye allows the doctor and his team to see pictures of the insides of blood vessels and hopefully would help them determine what the dark spot was in Adrien's brain. We agreed to the procedure, but unfortunately, he still did not have an answer for what he was seeing.

Adrien remained in the hospital for another day as they ran more tests, but still no answers came back. All the time our family and friends were praying with us that whatever it was would be healed. With no real answers, they released Adrien from the hospital, but the nonstop headaches continued.

Eventually, we were sent to the Cleveland Clinic to meet with a specialist. Another CAT scan was run. This time the brain specialist had some answers. He told us that Adrien had a cavernous angioma, which was a cluster of some smaller veins that were malformed and had been bleeding. We could have been discouraged by this news, but instead we now knew specifically what to pray for.

Seven years went by with no change. Adrien continued to deal with differing degrees of headaches that wouldn't stop. By this time, she was working at our company and was part of a voluntary meeting we were having on hearing from the Holy Spirit in the workplace. Our life insurance agent and friend, Mark, who had been a part of the group and had started healing rooms in Grand Rapids, Michigan, was leading the meeting.

Over the past few years, Mark and I had spent many hours discussing our testimonies and how God was working in our lives and businesses. We had prayed together on many occasions, and he asked if he could come in and present this material to anyone who would like to hear. He was considering doing this at other companies and wanted to try it out with us first.

Halfway through this meeting, he used an analogy of Adrien suffering from headaches to make a point, not knowing this was, in fact, something she was suffering from. I felt the Holy Spirit prompt me to tell Mark that Adrien had been battling headaches for seven years, so I did. He immediately asked if he could pray for her. She said yes. We all stretched out our hands toward her, and he placed his hands on her head and prayed for the removal of the cavernous angioma, the headaches, and the total healing of her brain.

During this prayer, they both felt heat where he had placed his hands, and her head pulsated in a strange way. Instantly, she was healed. No more headaches. After seven years of nonstop head pain, Adrien was completely healed! Praise God! God had moved right there in the middle of that meeting in the conference room at our workplace.

After the healing, Adrien said she had forgotten what it felt like to live pain free. The pain had become her normal. Mark made sure to inform her to stand firm in the healing because the enemy would try to cause doubt and take the healing away.

Later that week, Adrien started to feel a headache come on. She immediately was reminded of Mark's words and confessed out loud that she was healed by Jesus' stripes and the enemy had no hold on her healing. She immediately felt relief in her head.

We as believers need to expect the unexpected. Wherever God's presence is welcome, He will be there with healing in His wings (Malachi 4:2) or whatever is needed to bring Him glory.

I do not believe that any ministry can be effective without prayer. Continually bathe your outreach in prayer. Pray to the Lord of the harvest that He will send workers into the harvest field to work alongside you. Pray for your employer, that you will receive favor from them. Pray for divine appointments with your coworkers and those within your sphere of influence. Be obedient to God when He nudges you. Put on His armor daily, and then go. Be salt and light!

[7]
LOVING OUR NEIGHBORS

JESUS HAS GIVEN us the command to love our neighbors (Mark 12:31). As we work through applying this word from Jesus to our lives, it becomes impossible not to take our outreach for His Kingdom into the marketplace.

> On one occasion an expert in the law stood up to test Jesus. "Teacher," he asked, "what must I do to inherit eternal life?" "What is written in the Law?" he replied. "How do you read it?"
>
> - LUKE 10:25-26

The phrase "expert in the law" is most likely not referring to a lawyer in today's sense of the word. It is referring to an expert in the Mosaic law. As an expert in the Mosaic law, the man quoted back to Jesus Deuteronomy 6:5 and Leviticus 19:18.

He answered, "'Love the Lord your God with all your heart and with all your soul and with all your strength and with all your mind'; and, 'Love your neighbor as yourself.'" "You have answered correctly," Jesus replied.... But he wanted to justify himself, so he asked Jesus, "And who is my neighbor?" In reply Jesus said: "A man was going down from Jerusalem to Jericho, when he was attacked by robbers. They stripped him of his clothes, beat him and went away, leaving him half dead. A priest happened to be going down the same road, and when he saw the man, he passed by on the other side. So too, a Levite, when he came to the place and saw him, passed by on the other side. But a Samaritan, as he traveled, came where the man was; and when he saw him, he took pity on him. He went to him and bandaged his wounds, pouring on oil and wine. Then he put the man on his own donkey, brought him to an inn and took care of him. The next day he took out two denarii and gave them to the innkeeper. 'Look after him,' he said, 'and when I return, I will reimburse you for any extra expense you may have.' Which of these three do you think was a neighbor to the man who fell into the hands of robbers?" The expert in the law replied, "The one who had mercy on him." Jesus told him, "Go and do likewise."

- LUKE 10:27-37

To get a full understanding of the above passage, we need to understand the relationship between the Samaritans and the Jewish people in Jesus' day. The Jews hated the Samaritans. The Jews thought the Samaritans to be half-breed, idol worshipers. They were half Jewish and half gentile—an ethnicity that developed after the Assyrian captivity of the northern kingdom of Israel in 721 B.C. Some of the Jewish people during that time stayed behind and intermarried with the Assyrians, creating the Samaritans.

In John 4:9, when Jesus was talking to the Samaritan woman at the well, John revealed to us that Jews did not associate with Samaritans. So, in Luke 10, as Jesus taught the good neighbor parable, He purposely included the Samaritan in the group of three men who encountered this robbed and beaten man to show that even someone we may despise is still our neighbor. It would be expected by most at the time of Christ for a Jewish priest, being a religious man, to do the neighborly thing, or even a Levite who would have been an expert in the law. But they both walked right by the distressed man while the Samaritan stopped, bandaged his wounds, and took him to safety.

Jesus then answered the law expert's question, not by describing someone to whom he would have been close, but by describing someone the expert most likely would have despised. This leads us to the conclusion that everyone we come in contact with is our neighbor, and we are to show God's love to them, not only in words, but in deeds as well.

LOVE THEM AND LET GOD DO THE REST

Over the years, as I have tried to understand how God wanted to use us in the marketplace to further His Kingdom, the parable of the good Samaritan has been the model I've frequently used in my marketplace ministry. It becomes easy to walk through life spending all our time in a small group of like-minded people. We become comfortable walking right by and ignoring people who have been beaten down by the enemy and left for dead.

When we see a person in need of Jesus and struggling, do we think or, possibly even worse, condemn them for the bad decisions that got them in a hard place of need? We are not called to stand there and cast verbal stones at people. We're called to take action, like the good Samaritan, and offer assistance. We are called to show them God's love.

The Samaritan didn't berate the person in need, telling him what a mess he was, that he was foolish for walking down the road and allowing himself to be beaten and robbed. Instead, he showed him love, not just through some kind words, but also through action.

When we are dealing with unbelievers in our workplace or sphere of influence, we are not called to give them a laundry list of everything we feel they are doing that is outside God's best for their lives. They are not yet followers of Jesus and are most likely not living by the standards He has set for us. The pastors at my church have explained it this way: You can't clean the fish before you have it in the boat.

We tend to want to do the Holy Spirit's job for Him, going out and trying to clean everyone up. Inside the family of those who have accepted Jesus as their Lord and Savior, of course, we have conversations concerning obedience to God, His call for us to act, and what He has commanded in His Word. Proverbs 27:17 says, "As iron sharpens iron, so one person sharpens another." But notice the verse does not say, "Iron sharpens copper," or "Iron sharpens wood." It says, "Iron sharpens iron." It is two of the same metals sharpening each other.

In the same way, as Christians, we build relationships with other Christians and do life together, sharpening each other. Know your audience when you're loving on those in your sphere of influence and be careful not to try to clean the fish before it is in the boat. It's only through our saving relationship with our Lord and Savior that any of us are made clean.

> All of us have become like one who is unclean, and all our righteous acts are like filthy rags.
>
> - ISAIAH 64:6

> As it is written: "There is no one righteous, not even one."
>
> - ROMANS 3:10

God made him who had no sin to be sin for us, so that in him we might become the righteousness of God.

- 2 CORINTHIANS 5:21

As we approach doing His work in the marketplace, we must always remain humble and remember we are no different than those to whom we reach out. The only difference is our saving relationship with Jesus. In our own strength, we will be ineffective in our outreach. In His strength, we can collectively change the world.

CHOOSE LOVE

So how do we effectively walk out the command to love our neighbor as ourselves? First, we must understand that the love God calls us to is not a feeling but a decision. We must make the decision to love our neighbor and then go about doing it with God's help.

There are different Greek words that translate into our word *love*. The Greek word used in Luke 10's parable is *agape*, which is the same Greek word used for *love* as described in 1 Corinthians 13:4–7:

Love is patient, love is kind. It does not envy, it does not boast, it is not proud. It does not dishonor others, it is not self-seeking, it is not easily angered, it keeps no record of wrongs. Love does not delight in evil but rejoices with the truth. It always protects, always trusts, always hopes, always perseveres.

As you read through the verses above, does this description of love read like a feeling we would get or a decision we would make?

As we are working to love our neighbors, which is anyone with whom we come into contact, we should memorize these verses so that they are imprinted on our hearts and flow out through our actions. It's a good idea to do a periodic mental check to see if we are obeying the command to love our neighbor. We can ask ourselves, "Is this love visible to those around me?"

Again, we are not capable of being perfect at demonstrating love in our own strength. As God's love works through you in this way, His light shines brightly, and people will naturally be drawn to you. In a self-centered world desperately in need of love, this kind of love becomes contagious.

The Holy Spirit will start to provide divine appointments for conversations with people who are curious about the differences in the way you live. People will notice something intriguing about how you live, something that is counterintuitive to what they see in the world. As they see this difference in you, they will begin to ask questions. This will open doors for conversations that can accomplish God's purposes. Using the Word of God as a sledgehammer to condemn and criticize people only hinders His work.

Over the years, as I have answered many questions about my relationship with God, sharing with others what God has done for me, I have gotten many interesting responses. The most common are: "I don't believe that's what makes you different. I know lots of Christians, and they are all hypocrites," "Wow, I feel something is missing in my life," or "I have been feeling like I need to get back to church."

Whatever their response is, if you feel as though the Holy Spirit has orchestrated the conversation, you should realize a door has been opened for you to pray and seek His direction in building a Christ-centered relationship with that individual.

HOW TO BE A NEIGHBOR

We need to do more than invite individuals to church and pass the baton off to the church staff. In many cases, our pastors and church staff are already overworked and underpaid. We need to invite people to our churches with the intention to follow through with them. Pick them up at their home, meet them in the lobby, and then sit with them in the service. Afterward, invite them out to lunch to share thoughts about the sermon or to answer questions. A new culture, even a church setting, can be intimidating. Make them comfortable.

Being a good neighbor is relational. If someone has never attended a church or may have been hurt by a local church, you may need to explain what to expect when they attend church or help address some of the hurts they've experienced before you feel led to invite them to church. Offer to meet with them at break or lunchtime to get to know them better. Build a relationship and answer questions. Create an atmosphere of safety for sharing.

If you are ministering to someone of the opposite sex, have another believer there with you, preferably someone of the same sex as the person you are meeting with. Accountability is crucial. Allow your ministry partner to take the lead, and you take a much lesser role. Direct them to others or a group that may also be seeking to learn more about having a relationship with God.

We have held what we call a nonbelievers Bible study at lunch. The goal of this study is to create a space where individuals can ask questions about God and the Bible. Usually, the people who attend have questions about who Jesus is and how that affects their lives. If you choose to conduct a similar gathering at your workplace, respect the company's time and do it during a scheduled break time, lunch period, or before work. Make sure you pray about whom God would have you ask to attend prior to making your invitations. Make sure they know this gathering is for people who want to know more about the Bible and God. Assure them that a doctorate in theology or even a basic knowledge of the Bible is not required. The only require-ment is an interest in knowing about the risen King.

Most people don't know a lot about the Bible. They have heard bits and pieces that seem confusing. Some may have attended church a few times, and they may have seen

Hollywood's portrayal of Bible stories, but in today's society it is becoming more common to run into people who have had nothing to do with either.

If possible, have another believer there with you at the nonbelievers Bible study so there are at least two followers of Jesus in the room. Have a planned scripture to discuss. Have material prepared. Share your story if appropriate. If they don't have a Bible, be prepared to give them one. Point them to specific scriptures to read. Then, discuss them. Genesis 1–3 and the book of John are both good places to start. Have them read a couple chapters a week and ask them to consider the following questions as they read:

- What does this story say about God?
- What does this story say about man?
- If this is true, what will I change in my life?

DON'T PASS THEM BY

Before people are going to come and ask us questions about the God we serve or be willing to do Bible studies, they have to see some evidence of how God is being lived out in our lives. If Monday through Friday, they see nothing different in how we act or react to things, why would they want to know God and all that He has to offer? If they don't see and feel His love working through us and into their lives as we build relationships with them, we are greatly reducing the impact we can have for His Kingdom.

Every day inside our sphere of influence and in the marketplace, we are surrounded by people who have been robbed and beaten up by the enemy. If we are not careful, like the priest and the Levite, we will intentionally or unintentionally walk right past them each day in our workplaces. People are in need of what Jesus has to offer and in need of a good Samaritan to show them the love He has to offer. People are dealing with health and family issues, broken homes, financial struggles, drug addictions, sexual sin, depression, and general hopelessness. And these are just a few ways the enemy attempts to steal, kill, and destroy. We must learn to better love our neighbors in the marketplace and be in sync with the Holy Spirit to act when we are called upon.

CALLED TO ACTION

I was walking through our shop years ago when I noticed an employee who looked depressed. He was a big burly, young man who I learned had a wife and two children. He was normally very upbeat and a very good employee. I had opportunities to work closely with him on a couple of projects and had built a good relationship with him. As I walked toward him, I sensed something was wrong. Then, when I stood next to him and began to ask him how he was doing, he began to break down. He expressed he didn't know what to do. He was overwhelmed, and things were not going well at home. I walked him into a conference room, shut the door, and allowed him to pour out what was going on in his life.

He had been working a side job along with working full-time at our company, and his wife and he were both exhausted. With two small children and working constantly, they had no time for each other. She had grown frustrated with their relationship and had had enough. It was evident how much he loved her and the kids, but he wasn't sure what to change or how to change it.

I shared with him some of the things Karen and I had to put in place to make sure we protected our alone time together. We discussed our spiritual responsibilities as fathers and husbands. I prayed for him and invited him to meet us at church with his family, which he did a couple weeks later. We then agreed to sit down and talk again on a break time in a week to see how things were going.

We met weekly for about a month. Then, our meetings transitioned to visiting for a moment when I stopped by his area.

About a year after our first meeting, he stopped me one day and asked if he could talk to me. We sat down, and he thanked me for what I had done for him and his wife. He was excited to tell me that they were renewing their wedding vows. He was so thankful for the counsel I had given him and the time I had spent encouraging him— so thankful that he asked me to perform their renewal ceremony. Unfortunately, we had a previous commitment, so I was unable to be there. I was honored that he had asked me to be a part of that ceremony but, most of all, thankful that his family life and marriage had been restored.

When he broke down that first day, I could have just listened, told him I'd pray for him, and moved on. I can only imagine how hollow and unhelpful those words, "I'll pray for you," must sound to people who are not in a relationship with God. But like the good Samaritan in the parable, we are called to action. The action that was needed in this case was spending time, giving encouragement, and an offering to babysit their children so they could get out and have some time alone.

Remember, I had built a relationship with him over time, and we had gotten to know each other. I was not some stranger who worked alongside him. I was a person who was engaged and noticed the people around me. It is so much easier to really be love in action to someone whose life you have made a point to be engaged with.

When people notice how you treat others, it can open a door for the Holy Spirit to use you as a vehicle to pour into their lives. None of us will ever be perfect in our actions in how we treat people inside or outside the workplace, but we should ask for God's help and do our best to represent Him well. As His ambassadors, we are called to be salt and light wherever He places us, and that includes the marketplace.

SALT AND LIGHT

During Jesus' time, salt had different uses. Two of the most common were related to food preservation and flavor enhancement. Jesus did not tell us we could be or may be the salt of the earth. He told us we are the salt of the earth.

> You are the salt of the earth. But if the salt loses its saltiness, how can it be made salty again? It is no longer good for anything, except to be thrown out and trampled underfoot. You are the light of the world. A town built on a hill cannot be hidden. Neither do people light a lamp and put it under a bowl. Instead they put it on its stand, and it gives light to everyone in the house. In the same way, let your light shine before others, that they may see your good deeds and glorify your Father in heaven.
>
> - MATTHEW 5:13-16

We are to act as preservatives, fighting alongside Jesus against the moral decay in our world. We can't just be salty when attending our weekly Sunday service and then lose our saltiness on Monday through Saturday by looking and acting like everyone else around us.

In the same way that salt has a positive impact on our food, we should have a positive impact for our heavenly Father within the sphere of influence He has placed us. People should be attracted to us because they see and feel the love of Christ flowing through us. As Christ flows through us, we illuminate a spiritual light, bringing hope to a dark and lost world.

> Do everything without grumbling or arguing, that you may become blameless and pure, "children of God without fault in a warped and crooked generation." Then you will shine among them like stars in the sky.
>
> - PHILIPPIANS 2:14-15

Over the years, people have told me they need to get out of their jobs because they are dark places and they are working with all kinds of unbelievers. They complain that their coworkers use foul language, have office affairs, discuss pornography, and participate in all kinds of dark activities. While there are some work situations God may want to remove you from, there are others where He has placed you to be a light.

> The light shines in darkness, and the darkness has not overcome it.
>
> - JOHN 1:5

Sometimes, you have to pray through difficult work situations. You might also consider that God has you right where He wants you. Consider that He may want you to bring His light to that dark place. This may sound difficult and perhaps even awkward. Having a job where everyone is a believer may sound easy. That you can leave work, sit around a campfire, and sing "Kumbaya," and roast marshmallows until you are taken to your heavenly home sounds perfect. However, as followers of Jesus, our walk will not always be easy. Look at Paul, the other apostles, or Jesus Himself. Each of their lives was anything but easy. But Jesus promised to never leave us or forsake us. He will always be right there alongside us.

> God has said, "Never will I leave you; never will I forsake you." So we say with confidence, "The Lord is my helper; I will not be afraid. What can mere mortals do to me?"
>
> - HEBREWS 13:5-6

DON'T JUST BE GOOD—BE GREAT!

In our Western culture and in this age, our persecution is not as threatening as it is in other cultures around the world. We may be called names, made fun of for our beliefs, or dumped from friend groups, but these are small prices to pay for sharing our faith as we serve and love God who has done everything for us.

Recently, I reread one of my favorite books on business, *Good to Great*, by Jim Collins. I had read it years ago when it first was published, but this time I read it with a few of my direct reports. As I read the first few words in chapter 1—"Good is the enemy of great"[1]—I felt as if God was saying to me, "This is true spiritually as well."

Now, this is a business book. The author wrote it from a business perspective. Yet the words took on a more spiritual meaning as I read them this second time. It was odd to me that I felt as though I was hearing from God while reading these words, so I stopped and prayed. I asked Him for clarity about what He was trying to tell me. What I felt He was showing me was that, in our Western society, once we are born again, we feel good, and we should, but we need to continue. We should not stop at good because that goodness quickly becomes territory for the enemy and his plans and desires for our lives and becomes the enemy of growth and spiritual greatness.

The enemy wants us to settle into a good life, ineffective spiritually and just muddling along, assured of where we will spend eternity but having little to no impact for the Kingdom of heaven while on Earth. He convinces us our lives are too busy to worry about outreach, or he tries to shake our confidence with sharing Christ, telling us that the responsibility belongs to the local church.

We feel good if we volunteer at church for an hour a week, in addition to attending a service. That is good enough and as far as many of us are willing to go. Taking our outreach into the marketplace, being sold out for Jesus, and having an impact for Him there is crazy. "I'm good with going to work, doing my job, and going home," we may say.

Again, the local church, when done right, should be a hub for outreach. And, yes, serving in your local church is important, but God desires for both our relationship with Him and our outreach for Him to be great, not just good.

Seek God's direction for your life and what great looks like. It may very well be serving in some sort of outreach through your local church body. Don't wait for your pastor to tell you what to do.

God has called us all to fulfill the Great Commission. Therefore, we need to go. When we go, we need to have a plan for what we are going to when we get to where we've been sent. If we expect our communities, marketplace, states, countries, and world to be spiritually great, we need to be about doing His business as His followers in all the nations. If we are willing to settle for good, it will always be an enemy of great. We must remember whom we serve and what we are capable of as His children. When we partner with Him, we need to dream big dreams and expect great things because spiritual greatness is what God wants for all of us.

> Now to him who is able to do immeasurably more than all we ask or imagine, according to his power that is at work within us, to him be glory in the church and in Christ Jesus throughout all generations, for ever and ever! Amen.
>
> - EPHESIANS 3:20-21

When we pray, "Your kingdom come, your will be done, on earth as it is in heaven" (Matthew 6:10), what we are praying for is a dramatically different looking world than the one we live in. We can't expect to pray this prayer and become complacent, waiting for God to transform everything. How much better would our world be if every follower of Jesus, regardless of denomination, was salty and let their light shine brightly while loving their neighbors who are everyone with whom they come into contact?

---

1. Jim Collins, *Good to Great* (New York: HarperCollins, 2001), 1.

[8]
BEING SPIRITUALLY ATTRACTIVE

IN MATTHEW 28:19, Jesus gave us the responsibility for going out to share the gospel wherever He has placed us. There is no disputing that there is nothing we can do to work our way into heaven and right relationship with God. They are gifts we just need to accept in faith, repenting and asking Jesus into our hearts, making Him Lord of our lives. What we need then to grab hold of is that it doesn't stop there. As His sons and daughters, we have work to do for and with Him. He tells us in Ephesians 2:10, "We are God's handiwork, created in Christ Jesus to do good works, which God prepared in advance for us to do."

God has given us differing gifts and positions in His Body, but there are certainly things He has revealed to us in the Scriptures that we are all called to do. One of those things is written in Jesus' Great Commission found in Matthew 28:19–20:

Therefore go and make disciples of all the nations, baptizing them in the name of the Father and of the Son and of the Holy Spirit, and teaching them to obey everything I have commanded you.

Once we are saved, we should realize there is nothing more important than our relationship with God, where we will spend eternity, and then bringing this realization to the world around us. We must recognize eternity matters for us all. *Eternity* is defined in the dictionary as "infinite or unending time" or "a state to which time has no application."[1] It's easy to get caught up in the busyness of the here and now and forget that this place is only temporary.

"Amazing Grace" is one of my favorite songs. I am always moved by the words, "When we've been there ten thousand years, bright shining as the sun, we've no less days to sing God's praise than when we first begun."[2] As a father of four children and an owner of three businesses, there have been times in my life when I have been so busy that I have wanted to coast spiritually. When that has happened, one of the things God has used to refocus me on His Kingdom purposes has been the two moving stanzas from "Amazing Grace." He uses them to remind me that most of us will spend less than one hundred years here on Earth before relocating to where we will spend eternity.

When followers of Jesus are called home to heaven, and they have been there ten thousand years, they will have no less days than when we got there to sing God's praise. The question I hope to cause your heart to cry out for is who will be there singing with us?

So many friends, loved ones, and coworkers are wandering the world lost and without the hope of Christ. God saw fit to search you out, to bring His grace and love and mercy into your life, and because you accepted His call by faith, you now have a seat with Him in heavenly places. You will not suffer an eternity separated from Him and His love. Wouldn't you want those around you to have this same access, this same eternal destiny?

Every day, we go into our workplaces or neighborhoods, and we spend time with people who are in need of a saving relationship with Jesus. Do we recognize the marketplace as a place to reach the lost and hurting who are far from Jesus? Or do we view the marketplace as merely a place to earn a living? How does God look at the marketplace? What would we see if we looked at it through his eyes?

Matthew 9:37–38 says,

> Then he said to his disciples, "The harvest is plentiful but the workers are few. Ask the Lord of the harvest, therefore, to send out workers into his harvest field."

If you are a follower of Jesus, you are one of the workers He describes in this verse. Charles Spurgeon, who preached in England in the 1800s and is often referred to as the "prince of preachers,"[3] said that Matthew 9:38 weighed on his heart more than any other text in the Bible.

He said it haunted him perpetually.[4] I had to ask myself, "How do I feel about that verse?"

Studies tell us that on average seven to eight of the people we work with are not attending church or reading the Bible on a regular basis. The U.S. Bureau of Labor Statistics reports the average American full-time worker works 42.5 hours per week (8.5 hours/day).[5] If you allow for a half-hour a day for travel time and a half-hour a day for a nonworking lunch, you end up with an average of fifty-four hours a week dedicated to work. That is approximately a third of our time each week.

Besides sleeping, there is no one thing many of us spend more time doing each week than working. For most of us, we spend as much time, possibly even more, each week with our coworkers than our family.

Over the years, Karen and I have seen godly men and women who have taken those hours in the workplace to be excellent examples in their work and in the Faith. They have had great impact for God's Kingdom. Salvations, emotional and physical healings, and answers to prayer don't need to be limited to the local church building. I believe God uses the local church as the launching pad for ministry into the marketplace and neighborhoods.

At one time or another, we have run into what I will call a "bull in a china shop" type Christian brother or sister. This person wields the Bible like a bull wields its body and horns in a fragile china shop, turning precious items into fragments of what they once were. Their intentions may very well be good, but somehow or another they end up crushing or angering people, causing those they hurt to put up walls to avoid future communication altercations. These bullish types do not achieve the desired result of drawing people closer to Jesus. Often, people give a wide berth to such well-meaning individuals as they charge down the aisleway, as opposed to entering into a purposeful conversation, let alone building a relationship.

I cannot encourage you enough to take the time to build relationships with people and to get to know them. Charging forcibly into interactions with others is not effective. As we come into contact with people in the marketplace or inside our sphere of influence, we should start with easygoing conversations that over time turn into purposeful conversations that will eventually turn into spiritual conversations. We must always follow the leading of the Holy Spirit and His promptings. He will help us move naturally through the stages of healthy relationship building so that, when they need assistance, we are in position to do what we have the power to do.

> Do not withhold good from those to whom it is due, when it is in your power to act.
>
> - PROVERBS 3:27

Showing God's love by reaching out and meeting people's needs can be a great doorway for more purposeful and spiritual conversations over time. Helping someone move or work on their car or house, providing a meal or groceries, are just a few ways we can help meet day-to-day needs as they arise. Inviting someone into your home who has no place to go for a holiday can also be effective.

Growing up, we always had extra people in our home over the holidays. Many times, during my young adulthood, I was engaged to pick up a guest who was unable to drive to our home so they could celebrate with our family. At the time, I was uncomfortable with this job, but as I grew older, I saw the value in what my parents were asking me to do. Now, with my own family, Karen and I have invited many people from our companies over to celebrate with us and our family when they had no place to go and no family in the area with whom to celebrate holidays.

Visiting people when they or a loved one are sick and in the hospital can also open doors. When we make ourselves available to serve God in this way, our motive should be one of love and genuine concern. Using these situations to force spiritual conversations can be off-putting. When we show love and genuine concern for others, we may be planting seeds that someone else will water and reap the harvest of at a future time.

At times, our actions may lead to more purposeful and spiritual conversations. We need to let the Holy Spirit lead. We need to be ready, but we should not make people feel as if they are our "project." When we are kind and help meet people's needs, they will notice and will find us spiritually attractive. They may ask why we care for them the way we do. This opens the door to share what we feel God has called us to do.

When we invest time and treasure in people and show them God's love, we put ourselves on a solid foundation for sharing spiritually with them when that opportunity arises. Our responses to their questions will have value because we've laid a loving foundation.

SPIRITUALLY ATTRACTIVE IN THE MARKETPLACE

In the marketplace, we can make ourselves attractive or very unattractive by how we act and perform our jobs. As we interact with others, our coworkers, supervisors, vendors, and customers should see something different about us other than the norm. They should also see excellence in our job performance.

When I was employed by my first employer, I remember a meeting with some of the upper management who were concerned about employee performance. They spoke of one problem employee, a believer in Christ, who shared his faith, they felt, too much. His job performance was poor due to all the time he spent sharing about Jesus.

As they were saying he was the worst employee, another person at the table chimed in about a couple professing Christians in his department who he felt were both lazy and unreliable. Knowing I was a Christian, someone looked at me and said, "We know you're a great worker, Tom. This doesn't apply to you, but you have to admit this doesn't look good."

I sat in silence as I really didn't know what to say. They were right. I had just never thought of them as

Christian underperformers. I only saw them as employees who were underperforming.

I remember leaving that meeting thinking, *Wow! Everything we do as Christians reflects on our Father in heaven and impacts our outreach.* We would do well to remember:

> Whatever you do, work at it with all your heart, as working for the Lord, not for human masters, since you know that you will receive an inheritance from the Lord as a reward. It is the Lord Christ you are serving.
>
> — COLOSSIANS 3:23-24

> May the favor of the Lord our God rest on us; establish the work of our hands for us—yes, establish the work of our hands.
>
> — PSALM 90:17

> Diligent hands will rule, but laziness ends in forced labor.
>
> — PROVERBS 12:24

> One who is slack in his work is brother to one who destroys.
>
> — PROVERBS 18:9

If we expect to be effective as marketplace missionaries and be spiritually attractive to people, we should seek to be excellent at our craft. As His sons and daughters, we are representing God as much by our actions in the marketplace as we are by our words. If we are lazy and don't produce or excel in the marketplace, our opportunity to have an effective outreach will be greatly diminished. I can't stress enough how important it is to be diligent and excel at the work our Lord has provided for us to do. We need to be thankful for the work He has provided us and pray that He would give us the ability and wisdom we need to find favor in our employer's eyes. This will benefit us both physically and spiritually in our marketplace.

Who are you most drawn to in the marketplace—an unproductive employee who comes in late and complains all the time or someone who is prompt, positive, kind, helpful, and excellent at what they do?

Even if you put the outreach part of the equation off to the side, we are not representing our Father in heaven if we are not applying ourselves to excellence at our workplace. God wants your outreach for Him to be effective, so it becomes important for you to ask Him to help you become excellent at your work. You should have an advantage over those who do not have the Holy Spirit deposited inside them.

I know this may sound strange, but God cares about every facet of our lives and does not leave us on our own as we go about doing His business. As we pray and ask for creative solutions to issues we encounter daily in our jobs, God can supply them.

Hudson Taylor, a missionary to China, had a saying. I've kept it on my office wall for decades. He said, "God's work done God's way will never lack God's provision." I have always believed this in the marketplace. If I am about God's business at work, He will provide the time for me to do what needs to be done.

One of the ways He has done that over the years is quickly bringing solutions to problems to the forefront of my mind—solutions that might otherwise take a long time to find. He helped me in this way one day when I was walking on our shop floor. I had stopped to ask one of our manufacturing engineers and a machinist how they were doing. They said that they were struggling, working all morning on an issue and had not been able to solve it. I asked them to tell me the problem they were having.

As they finished telling me, something came to the forefront of my mind. It was an odd thought, an idea that you normally wouldn't consider or think would be causing this problem. I took the risk of sounding stupid and asked them to look at a certain item to see if it was causing the problem. They both looked at me with a puzzled look, as if I were crazy. I smiled and asked them to humor me and check it.

When I stopped back by to see them twenty minutes later, the machine was up and running, and the issue was solved. Had the Holy Spirit not brought the solution to me at that point, I would have most likely spent all day working with them to find the issue.

If we are willing to partner with God and do His work in the marketplace, He will partner with us, helping to make us more productive with the physical work we have to do. Over the many years in my journey with God, I have found that you cannot out-give Him in any area of your life.

> God is able to bless you abundantly, so that in all things at all times, having all that you need, you will abound in every good work.
>
> – 2 CORINTHIANS 9:8

---

1. "Eternity," *Dictionary*, https://www.dictionary.com/browse/eternity?s=t/.
2. John Newton, "Amazing Grace," *Timeless Truths*, https://library.timelesstruths.org/music/Amazing_Grace/. The copyright of "Amazing Grace" is in public domain.
3. "Charles Spurgeon," *Wikipedia*, https://en.wikipedia.org/wiki/Charles_Spurgeon/.
4. Charles Haddon Spurgeon, "Harvest Men Wanted," *The Spurgeon Center*, https://www.spurgeon.org/resource-library/sermons/harvest-men-wanted#flipbook/. The words appeared in Spurgeon's sermon of August 17, 1873. The sermon appeared in the *Metropolitan Tabernacle Pulpit Volume 19*. It was sermon number 1,127.
5. U.S. Bureau of Labor Statistics, "Average hours employed people spent working on days worked by day of week, 2018 annual averages," *U.S. Bureau of Labor Statics*, https://www.bls.gov/charts/american-time-use/emp-by-ftpt-job-edu-h.htm/.

[9]
BECOMING A MARKETPLACE MISSIONARY

KAREN and I have spent the past thirty-plus years working for others as well as starting and running our own businesses. Early in my business life, I felt God calling me to the mission field, which for me is the marketplace. Over the years, I have seen God use godly men and women in the marketplace to have an amazing impact for His Kingdom. Salvations, emotional and physical healings, and answers to prayer don't need to be limited to the local church building. I believe God uses the local church as the epicenter for ministry into the marketplace and neighborhoods.

If 70 to 80 percent of Americans are not attending church on a regular basis, we have to get out of our comfort zone and take the church to them. To see our cities, states, and nations change, we cannot sit idly by and watch our pastors or local church leaders bear the responsibility for change alone. As followers of Jesus, we are the church with the capital C. We are ambassadors for the Kingdom of God, and God wants to partner with us to change our communities one person at a time. In part, our pastors' job is to teach and equip us to go out into our world to be difference makers for Jesus, making disciples of men and women.

Knowing God has called us into the marketplace—not just to provide a service for our employers and customers, but also to act as His missionaries—is just the beginning. Our enemy does not want us to take what we know and put a plan in place to have the greatest outreach impact we can for the Kingdom of God. Satan will do everything within his power to make sure we are ineffective in reaching the lost. He will lie to us, telling us we are too busy, not talented enough, not good enough, and so on. He may very well be telling you some of these lies as you read this. If you are feeling this way, rebuke the enemy and pray aloud:

Father,
Your Word says that I can do everything through
You who gives me strength (Philippians 4:13). I
draw my strength from You and thank You for the
vision You'll give me for my outreach in the
marketplace.

Thank You, that as I partner with You, I will have
the necessary time and resources required to be
effective in doing Your work in my marketplace.

In Jesus' name, I rebuke the enemy and his lies
about my ability to accomplish all You have created
me for, and I stand firm in what Your Word tells
me. I am your handiwork, created in Christ Jesus to
do good works, which You prepared in advance for
me to do (Ephesians 2:10). Amen.

A famous quote by Ben Franklin says, "If you fail to plan, you are planning to fail."[1]

We need to pray and put a plan in place for working in the marketplace. As we put our plans in place, we must continue to listen to the direction of the Holy Spirit, making any necessary adjustments as He leads us. A sample plan to be put in place and worked out could contain some of the following items.

PRAYER

We discussed prayer at length in chapter 6. Your plan needs to start with and be bathed in prayer. Set aside specific times to pray for your marketplace and those with whom you work. Possibly set aside one lunch period a week where you skip eating lunch to fast and pray. If lunch doesn't work for you, get creative. Find a time that does work and begin.

Try to get in the habit of praying as you are walking into the workplace each day and as you are leaving for home. On your way in, pray that God's favor will be upon your work that day and that, as divine appointments arise,

He will provide you with the words and actions He desires for you to deliver. On your way out, thank Him for the job He has provided you and the company you work for. Pray for any individuals you may have had conversations with that day as He brings them to mind.

Going into your weekly prayer time with a prayer journal and some specific things to pray for can be helpful. This prayer time should be geared toward the people you work with and how you can better love on them and reach them for Jesus.

SEARCH FOR THE REMNANT

As you begin your prayer time and focus on the marketplace, you should be looking for other followers of Jesus to partner with. As I mentioned before, setting a weekly time apart to pray for your marketplace is important, and finding others to join with you should also be a focus.

Working with other brothers and sisters in Christ in our outreach is a biblical principle. Jesus sent the seventy-two out in pairs in Luke 10. In Ecclesiastes 4:12, He tells us of the strength we gain when we work together: "Though one may be overpowered, two can defend themselves, a cord of three strands is not quickly broken."

As long as there is unity, there is strength as we gather together to pray and be about the Father's business.

I have found over the years this also adds accountability and consistency to the weekly prayer meeting. It allows you to cover more ground if those you are gathering with work in other areas of the same company. You are not all coming into contact with and building relationships with the same people.

As you gather together and pray for individuals, share different ideas on how to best show them God's love. We are definitely stronger and more effective when we stand with other brothers and sisters in Christ, doing battle for those who are lost and hurting.

Don't allow the enemy to cause division in your group over small issues. Stay focused on outreach for God. It is likely you will be meeting with people who attend different local churches. The enemy will want to distract you with things like pre-tribulation rapture versus post-tribulation rapture. Agree to disagree on items like that. Don't allow such differences to disrupt the unity you have around your focus on your marketplace mission field.

Finally, remember to put on the armor of God (Ephesians 6:10–18).

BUILD RELATIONSHIPS AND BE SENSITIVE TO DIVINE APPOINTMENTS

We need to be sensitive to the Spirit and not ignore hurting people as we were instructed by the parable of the good Samaritan. If we are making a plan to partner with God as a marketplace missionary, we must have our spiritual antennae up and be ready and willing to love our neighbors. For us to be effective in the marketplace, this principle must move from our heads to our hearts. It can't just be something we know; it has to become something we consistently do.

I can read all the health and fitness books and magazines I want, learning everything there is to know about the proper diet and exercise to change the way my body looks. Until I put them into practice, nothing about my body will change. Having the spiritual knowledge about what we should be doing and actually doing it are obviously two totally different things.

Loving your neighbor in the marketplace is not always easy. At times, we are called to love and pray for people we may not get along with. We need to remember we are not the ones deciding with whom these divine appointments are set. It is the Creator of the universe, our heavenly Father, who is directing our paths.

As we work and interact with people to build relationships on a daily basis, we ought to be looking for conversations over time that move from easygoing to purposeful and then on to spiritual. Be on the lookout for needs to meet. If you are meeting and praying with a group, team up together as a group to meet these needs where appropriate. Maybe someone you are working with has a car issue and one of your fellow prayer partners is a great mechanic. In that case, maybe they could show God's love by helping the person repair their car.

We should all be one body working together with the same goals in mind, and those would be the goals of our Father in heaven.

MAKE DISCIPLES

We need to keep in mind that the Bible does not call us to make converts but disciples. In the Great Commission, God calls us to go and make disciples of every nation, teaching them everything He has commanded us (Matthew 28:19–20). The local church definitely plays a very large role in this, but we can't shy away from our responsibility. We personally have to make disciples as well.

You may at some point have an opportunity to do a Bible study with some of the individuals you have walked beside in the marketplace after they have become new believers. You may be able to do this at lunch at your company if they allow that or before or after work.

Start putting a plan together for what it would look like for you to lead a new believers Bible study group. How would you disciple them over three, six, or twelve months? Would you meet weekly or biweekly?

As discussed in chapter 7, a good place to start would be Genesis 1–3 and the book of John. Have those in your Bible study read and then discuss two chapters a week for twelve weeks of meetings, totaling twenty-four chapters of reading.

If you are concerned that you won't be able to answer all the questions they may have, be honest with them before the first gathering and tell them that you do not have all the answers. Together, you can pray and work alongside them to find answers to those specific questions.

You should prepare and be ready to lead the conversation around the chapters you have read each week. Bible commentaries can be helpful when preparing for the lesson. Remind those participating in the study to ask themselves the following questions as they read the chapters:

- What does this say about God?
- What does this say about me and mankind?
- After reading this passage, what will I change in my life?

Encourage them to share what they are learning with others just as you are taking time to share with them. As you disciple them, spend some time discussing how God has called them to go and share their faith and what this may look like for them. Remember, He has called us to go and make disciples for the purpose of their going and making disciples.

THE LOCAL CHURCH

When they are ready, help the people you are discipling get plugged into local churches you trust. It is a good idea to have a few churches in mind for them to try as local churches are not "one size fits all."

You will need to be sensitive to the individual and not push too hard at the start. Some people are ready and excited right away to go to church. Others may have been hurt by a local church, and it may take a little time for God to do a work in their lives before they are ready.

Being a part of a vibrant, Bible-teaching, Jesus-centered local church in unison with a group of believers you are doing life and church with is a blessing. I feel privileged to attend my local church, serving alongside and sitting under the teaching of my pastor, Lee Cummings. As I have attended Radiant Church for the past nineteen years, I have been challenged to continue to grow and become more effective in my outreach.

If we all embrace God's call for us to go and partner with Him in reaching the lost and hurting, we will not only be making a positive difference in the world as we see it today. We will also have an impact on the Kingdom of heaven for eternity.

Second Corinthians 5 tells us there will come a day when we will all appear before the judgment seat of Christ. When I get there, I don't want to hear, "There was so much more I wanted to do with you to reach the lost and the hurting." When I get there, no different than you, I'm sure, I desire to hear, "Well done, good and faithful servant."

As a body of believers, followers of Jesus, we have an opportunity to change our view of the marketplace. We cannot simply view it as a place to go and earn a living while acting ethically among our coworkers. We must expand our view and attempt to see the marketplace like God does, as a mission field, full of lost and hurting people in need of His grace and mercy. As local church attendance continues to dwindle, we should obtain a mindset that we are all missionaries sent to share the good news wherever He has placed us.

For over thirty years now, I have felt Him calling me to the marketplace, not just to earn a living, but also as a place to do ministry. The relationships we build and partner with God to have a spiritual impact on in the marketplace will echo through the halls of heaven for eternity. May they echo in a mighty way on behalf of the marketplace mission field He has provided you to influence.

I pray that the Lord of the harvest will send out workers into His harvest field.

They overcame him by the blood of the Lamb, and by the word of their testimony; and they loved not their lives unto the death.

- REVELATION 12:11, KJV

"'The Lord bless you and keep you; the Lord make his face shine on you and be gracious to you; the Lord turn his face toward you and give you peace.'"

- NUMBERS 6:24-26

---

1. "Benjamin Franklin: Quotes: Quotable Quote," *goodreads*, https://www.goodreads.com/quotes/460142-if-you-fail-to-plan-you-are-planning-to-fail/.

.